The Key to Joyce is Language

One day in Zurich, while writing **Ulysses**, Joyce encountered his friend Frank Budgen. Joyce looked unusually pleased with himself. He seemed to have had a successful day.

Joyce had a musical ear and the sound of prose was always extremely important to him. A golden rule for the reader is **when in doubt, read aloud.** There is also in Joyce a rich vein of humour, even at the blackest moments. There are plenty of good old-fashioned belly laughs, but also some sly oblique smiles that reward only the careful reader.

A Rigorous Realist

James Joyce was possessed by an unswerving devotion to his art throughout his life. Undeterred by poverty, illness, family problems or world wars, he never wavered in the service of his often misunderstood genius.

Language was his raw material, and he applied to it the kind of extreme tests and standards more usually expected of poetry. He displayed the same standards of integrity in dealing with his subject matter, an uncompromising realist writing of areas of human experience previously regarded as too mean, too personal, too intimate or too risqué to be made the subject of art. In particular, he blew away the cobwebs surrounding the Victorian treatment of sexuality and presented it in an honest manner that was revolutionary. In so doing, he heroically expanded the frontiers of human spiritual development.

Dublin 1904

Joyce, above all else, is the quintessential modernist recorder of city life.

He first left Dublin in 1904 and did not visit again after 1912. Yet, for the remaining 28 years of his life in exile, he wrote about nothing else but Dublin.

It became for him a city frozen in time – the Edwardian Dublin of 1904 with its horse-drawn cabs, gas lamps and British soldiers, a city of some 500,000 souls where respectability and the subversive went hand in hand.

With the Dublin Mountains as a backdrop, the sweep of the bay half circles the metropolis like a sleeper's arms, and the River Liffey – Joyce's Anna Livia – rises in the foothills and meanders in a wide arc before flowing through the city to the sea. The Irish name for Dublin is **Baile Atha Cliath** or the town of the ford of the Hurdles, indicating a convenient place for crossing the river.

Dublin was founded by the Vikings over 1,000 years ago (although a settlement of some sort is indicated on Ptolemy's map many centuries earlier).

Splendidly brilliant in the 18th century, when for a brief period an independent parliament was established in the capital, Dublin's glory did not long survive the extinction of that parliament by the Act of Union in 1800.

The great town houses of the aristocracy were abandoned, first to the rising Catholic bourgeoisie, and then to tenement occupation.

This is Joyce's description of Henrietta Street, which had once been Dublin's finest Georgian street.

...a horde of grimy children populated the street. They stood or ran in the roadway or crawled up the steps before the gaping doors, or squatted like mice upon the threshold...He picked his way deftly through all that minute vermin-like life and under the shadow of the gaunt spectral mansions in which the old nobility of Dublin had roistered.

Dublin's "old nobility" was the arrogant and unrepresentative Protestant élite, far removed from the Gaelic and Catholic Ireland from which James Joyce sprang.

Some idea of the grandiose notions of these past grandees (or so-called "Ascendancy") can be seen on the city map. One of the great 18th century landowners, Henry Moore, Earl of Drogheda, literally built his name across the centre of Dublin.

The Dublin Obsession

Joyce absorbed much anecdotal information on walks round Dublin with his father John Stanislaus Joyce. "There was Buck Whaley the 18th century rake who walked to Jerusalem and played handball on its walls for a bet, and Skin the Goat, accomplice in a sensational political assassination, and Francy Higgins the sham squire . . . " These colourful eccentrics were later to flit though the pages of Joyce's works.

Even as a child, Joyce had a prodigiously retentive memory and an enquiring mind, as his father remarked.

When in middle age Joyce was asked, would he ever return to Dublin? "Have I ever left it?" he replied. "When I die, Dublin will be found engraved upon my heart."

Despite his love for the city, Joyce was ruthlessly unsentimental about it. He told a bemused audience in Trieste before the First World War: "Dubliners strictly speaking are my fellow countrymen, but I don't care to speak of our 'dear dirty Dublin' as they do. Dubliners are the most hopeless, useless and inconsistent race of characters I have ever come across on the island or on the continent. This is why this English Parliament is full of the greatest windbags in the world."

Dublin's Archivist

IF DUBLIN WERE EVER TO BE DESTROYED, IT COULD BE REBUILT FROM THE PAGES OF MY WORKS.

Well, the boast is not strictly true. There is very little architectural detail of the city in Joyce's writings. He was more interested in the lives of Dublin's citizens than the buildings which housed them. It was the moral and psychological landscape of the town that fascinated him.

"Joyce, Joyce, why he's nobody – from the Dublin docks: no family, no breeding." (George Moore, Irish novelist, in 1922)

James Joyce was born 2 February 1882, not in the Dublin slums, as some have claimed, but at 41 Brighton Square in the quiet, exclusive red-bricked Victorian suburb of Rathgar.

Initially, the family circumstances were comfortable and, at least in a musical sense, cultivated. Both his parents possessed fine voices and an interest in opera.

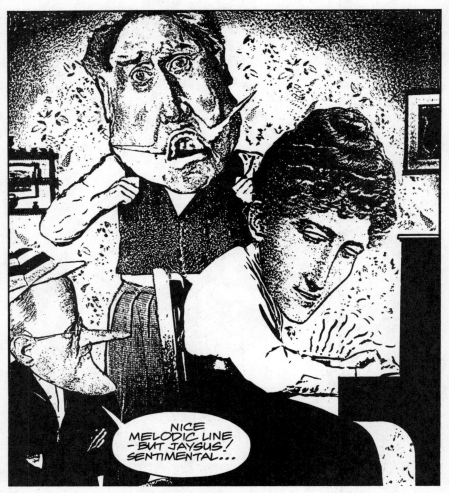

Joyce included many popular Victorian ballads and opera extracts in his fiction, but invariably with irony.

His father John Stanislaus Joyce was at first a model parent to the child, joining in nursery games, engaging in childlike prattle and spinning yarns for the fascinated boy.

Joyce remembered this "moocow" and used it to open his first novel, **A Portrait of the Artist as a Young Man**.

His mother, Mary Jane Murray, daughter of a Longford wine merchant, was a quiet, peace-loving woman with a gentle and refined nature who did not realize at first that she had married a drunkard and given birth to a genius. Mr Murray disapproved strongly of his daughter's friendship with dissolute John Joyce and he tried to prevent the engagement.

Dante's Hell

Joyce's education began at home under the guidance of a jilted aunt once removed, Mrs Hearn Conway. "Auntie" mispronounced as "Dante" was appropriate, since Mrs Conway (fictionalized as Dante Riordan in Joyce's **A Portrait of the Artist as a Young Man**) had a Dantesque obsession with hell. She took James and his younger brother Stanislaus to the National Gallery to show them a painting called "The Last Day".

"Pull out his eyes..."

At the age of 4 or 5, James announced he was going to marry Eileen Vance whose father kept the local chemist shop. Dante, shocked because Eileen was Protestant, chased him round the table. Mrs Joyce as usual attempted to placate her.

This incident too appears in **A Portrait.**

School Days

In September 1888, at age six-and-a-half, Joyce was taken by his parents to the great Jesuit boarding school in Co. Kildare, Clongowes Wood College.

(*peach = sneak or inform)

Little James was the youngest boy in the school.

HOW OLD ARE YOU?

HALF PAST SIX.

This became for a time his nickname at Clongowes.

Although a good student, Joyce felt himself an outsider, not excelling at team games. He became quite a good runner, which satisfied his idea of being an individualist loner. The school punishment book records his chatisement for "vulgar language" and other minor offences. Erring students were slapped with a hard leather instrument called a pandybat.

Meanwhile, the Joyce family fortunes were in decline, thanks to his father's addiction to politics and drink. An ironic summary of his father's occupations is given at the end of **A Portrait**.

A medical student, an oarsman, a tenor, an amateur actor, a shouting politician, a small landlord, a small investor, a drinker, a good fellow, a story teller, somebody's secretary, something in a distillery, a tax gatherer, a bankrupt and at present a praiser of his own past.

John Stanislaus Joyce had done brilliantly in his first year at medical school at Cork, but then drifted into a more glamorous career as the star of college theatricals and sporting events.

Subsequent failures were cushioned by a series of family bequests which he eventually succeeded in squandering, although it lent at least some stability to the early years of his marriage.

His grandfather, John O'Connell (reputed to be a cousin of the great 19th century politician Daniel O'Connell, champion of Catholic emancipation and known as "The Liberator"), gave him the enormous sum of £1,000 for his 21st birthday on 4 July 1870.

He promptly ran off to join the French forces in the Franco-Prussian War which broke out the same month. His outraged mother set off in pursuit, intercepted him in London and brought him back to Cork.

A series of Fenian (extreme republican) escapades led his mother to remove them both to Dublin in 1874/5. Here he attempted a business career, investing in the Dublin and Chapelizod Distillery Company organized by a fellow Cork man, Henry Alleyn.

Echoes of this event went into **Dubliners**, **A Portrait**, **Ulysses** and **Finnegans Wake**.

John Joyce next turned his attention to politics. As secretary of the United Liberal Club in Dublin, he organized for the general election of 18 April 1880 so skilfully that he managed to unseat the last two Conservative MPs in Dublin, Sir Arthur Guinness (the brewer) and James Stirling.

I was the cock of the walk that day and I never will forget it. I was complimented by everybody. I got 100 guineas from each of the members. My God, it was three o'clock in the morning and the excitement was great and I was the hero of it all because they said it was I won the election. By God Almighty, such drinking of champagne I never saw in my life. We could not wait to draw the corks, we slapped them against the marble-topped counter.

This oft-repeated tale of triumph made its way into **Finnegans Wake**.

Basking in the glory of his victory, John Joyce married Mary Jane Murray in the next month, 5 May 1880. As prolific in parenthood as he was prodigal in life, he fathered thirteen children, of whom ten survived infancy. James Joyce was the second son to be born, but the oldest of the surviving children. John Stanislaus embarked on the policy of mortgaging his property to sustain his lifestyle.

BY THE TIME THE LAST CHILD, MABEL (BABY) ARRIVED IN NOVEMBER 1897 THERE WERE TEN MORTGAGES TO MATCH THE TEN CHILDREN!

The Rise and Fall of Parnell

Besides begetting children, John Stanislaus fell under the spell of the
nationalist leader, Charles Stewart Parnell – aristocratic, Protestant,
Anglo-Irish but immensely popular with the ordinary people as the
"Uncrowned King of Ireland".
Parnell's spectacular rise compensated somewhat for the Joyce family's
downward spiral.

By the autumn term of 1891, finances were so precarious that James, now aged 8, was withdrawn from Clongowes.

PARNELL TOO WAS MARKED FOR DESTRUCTION!

Parnell's ruin was accomplished by the public disclosure of his adultery with the wife of a political colleague, Captain William O'Shea. Everyone had already known of this affair.

AFTER ALL, ADULTERY AND FOXHUNTING WERE THE PRINCIPAL PASTIMES OF THE BRITISH RULING CLASSES – THEN AS NOW!

The Parnell catastrophe contributed to a further descent into squalor for the Joyces. It affected the young James profoundly. Parnell became a mythic figure incorporated into all his prose works.

The destruction of Parnell, pictured through the stories of John Stanislaus and his cronies, inspired Joyce's first published work. This was a broadside poem, "Et tu, Healy", aimed at the betrayers of Parnell, and in particular his treacherous lieutenant, Tim Healy.

No copies survived, only a short fragment remembered by Joyce's brother Stanislaus.

his quaint perched aerie on the crags of time
where the rude din of this century
can trouble him no more.

Mr Joyce claimed to have sent a copy to the Vatican library for the Pope's personal edification. This copy also has not been traced.

Parnell's disgrace gave John Stanislaus a convenient alibi for drinking. The family moved ever closer to the slums of the north inner city.

The family's wretched few belongings always included the gilded ancestral portraits and the Galway Joyces' coat-of-arms with its scarcely appropriate motto **Mors Aut Honorabilis Vita** – death before dishonour.

James and Stanislaus were now sent to the Christian Brothers' school in North Richmond Street. A chance meeting with the former rector of Clongowes College, Fr Conmee, now rector of Belvedere, led to an offer of a place at this other fine Jesuit school.

This incident also appears in Joyce's *A Portrait*.

A.M.D.G.

Joyce once again received the education proper to a "young gentleman". But this was in obvious contradiction to the life he was actually forced to lead at home. He composed little school essays on topics like "Manners Maketh Man" or "Trust not Appearances", always beginning them with the Jesuit motto A.M.D.G. – **Ad Malorem Dei Gloriam** – To the Greater Glory of God.

Some of these essays still survive in their childish notebooks in American rare book collections. They consist of a melodious collection of clichés, giving no hint of the literary greatness to come. However, a revolution was taking place internally as the adolescent started to question the values on which Irish society was built, in which comfortable platitudes often papered over the horror of poverty and domestic strife. He continued to do brilliantly in an academic sense, winning a series of prizes in state examinations, before eventually being admitted to what is now University College Dublin where he took an Arts Degree course.

Night Town

Sexually as well as intellectually precocious, Joyce had begun to experiment with prostitutes in his early teens. He lived near Dublin's then thriving red light district, known locally as Monto (after Montgomery Street, one of its principal thoroughfares) or "Night Town", as Joyce calls it in **Ulysses**.

Joyce scrupulously records these encounters in **A Portrait of the Artist as a Young Man**.

Defender of Ibsen

Joyce showed himself a brilliant outsider with a gift for oratory when he read a paper, "Drama and Life", at the University College debating society, extolling the virtues of the great realist Norwegian playwright, Henrik Ibsen (1828-1906). Ibsen was deemed a dangerous subversive and Joyce's public reading had initially been banned by the authorities.

Stephen Hero, an early draft novel (c.1905), gives a flavour of that evening's polemical performance.

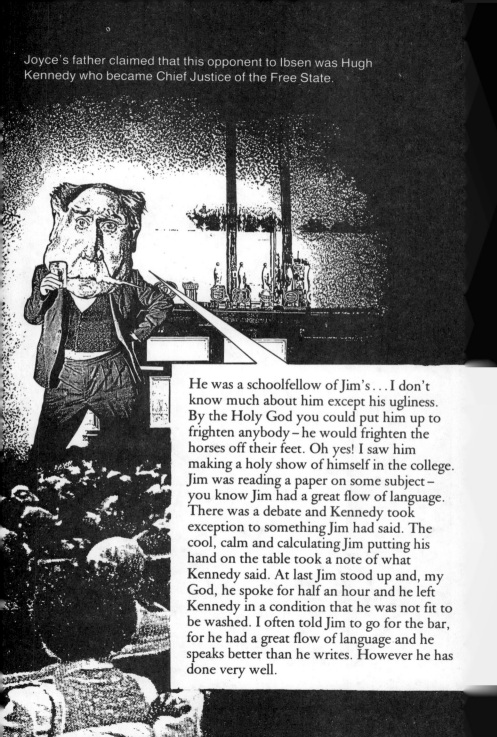

Joyce's father claimed that this opponent to Ibsen was Hugh Kennedy who became Chief Justice of the Free State.

He was a schoolfellow of Jim's . . . I don't know much about him except his ugliness. By the Holy God you could put him up to frighten anybody – he would frighten the horses off their feet. Oh yes! I saw him making a holy show of himself in the college. Jim was reading a paper on some subject – you know Jim had a great flow of language. There was a debate and Kennedy took exception to something Jim had said. The cool, calm and calculating Jim putting his hand on the table took a note of what Kennedy said. At last Jim stood up and, my God, he spoke for half an hour and he left Kennedy in a condition that he was not fit to be washed. I often told Jim to go for the bar, for he had a great flow of language and he speaks better than he writes. However he has done very well.

Joyce as Reviewer

Having completed his degree, Joyce left for Paris in November 1902, avowedly to study medicine. He tried his hand at book reviewing for the newspapers, but his standards proved too inflexible to make a commercial success of it.

A story is told which is typical of Joyce. C. Lewis Hind, editor of the **Academy**, gave him a book for trial review. Joyce savaged it and Hind complained.

Joyce had already developed a taste for biting the hand that fed him. During the year or so of Joyce's review work, one constant theme emerges in his articles.

The Young Bohemian

In Paris, Joyce was constantly hungry, cold and in debt. He sent harrowing letters home to Dublin, which succeeded in galvanizing his impoverished family into sending him whatever funds they could scrape together. Even in exile, he needed to feel he was still the centre of attention for his family at home. Here is his mother writing to him at Christmas, 1902.

My Dear Jim, if you are disappointed in my letter and if, as usual, I fail to understand what you would wish me to explain, believe me it is not from any want of a longing desire to do so and speak the words you want, as you often said I am stupid and cannot grasp the great thoughts which are yours much as I desire to do so. Do not wear your soul out with tears but be as usually brave and look hopefully to the future. Let me have a letter by return and for God's sake take care of your health and if you get the little stove be very careful with it.

This combination of intellectual submission and maternal solicitude was a recurring pattern in his dealings with women. He came home for Christmas, but returned to Paris where his litany of starvation continued. His capacity for suffering was matched by a talent for buoyant recuperation.

Dear Mother... your money order for 3 shillings/4 pence was very welcome as I hadn't eaten for 42 hours. I hope these spells of starvation won't ruin my digestion... I could buy a little oil stove to cook macaroni when I am hard beat... I sleep off part of my hunger in the mornings... Are you selling things to feed me?

...ps here's a jaunty air for the flute, UPA-UPA!

Mary Joyce was by now seriously ill, and on Good Friday, 10 April 1903, Joyce was summoned home to Dublin by his father's famous telegram which reappears in **Ulysses**. "Mother dying, come home, Father."

She had cancer, but lingered until 13 August, Joyce sometimes soothing her by playing the piano and singing for her Yeats's song "Who Goes with Fergus", as Stephen Dedalus does in **Ulysses**. Throughout that novel, Stephen is haunted by the ghost of his mother, just as Joyce himself was in real life.

As Mary Joyce's health declined, the pace of her husband's drinking became more furious. One night he came home, drunk and exasperated by his wife's condition, burst into her room and shouted at her.

Joyce's younger brother made to attack him.

Joyce managed to separate them and lock his father in an adjoining bedroom. The scene was reduced to farce a few minutes later, when John Stanislaus was seen shinning down a drainpipe and heading off again for the pubs.

James Joyce had by now totally abandoned the religion of his birth and he obstinately rejected his mother's pleas that he should go to confession and make his Easter duty by attending Mass. At her deathbed, an officious uncle noted that neither James nor Stanislaus was kneeling.

Joyce later embroidered the incident in **Ulysses**.

The whole family was distraught in bereavement, but especially the youngest child Mabel, still only 9 years old. Stanislaus Joyce recounts how she would steal upstairs to hide her grief. James, for once, allowed his real humanity to be revealed. "I remember him sitting on the top step of the first flight of stairs with his arm around her, talking to her in a very matter of fact voice."

You must not cry like that, because there is no reason to cry. Mother is in heaven. She is far happier now than she has ever been on earth, but if she sees you crying it would spoil her happiness. You must remember that when you feel like crying. You can pray for her if you wish. Mother would like that. But you mustn't cry anymore.

This tender concern for his sister did not blur his literary judgment. A few days after the funeral, he came across a packet of his parents' love letters. He took them outside to the garden, and having read them remarked laconically . . .

He handed them over to Stanislaus, who scrupulously burned them without prying into their contents.

All was grist to Joyce's mill, and he remembered his poignant rummaging amongst his mother's pathetically few possessions when he came to evoke her shade in the opening chapter of **Ulysses**.

Her secrets. Old feather fans, tasselled dancecards, powdered with musk, a gaud of amber beads in her locked drawer. A birdcage hung in the sunny window of her house when she was a girl. She heard old Royce sing in the pantomime of 'Turko the Terrible' and laughed with others when he sang

   I am the boy
   That can enjoy
   Invisibility

Phantasmal mirth, folded away: muskperfumed

Fateful Year, Fateful Day

As one important woman left Joyce's life, another entered it. On 10 June 1904, James Joyce was walking along Nassau Street, when a beautiful young woman caught his attention.

Her name was Nora Barnacle, a young Galway girl who worked as a chambermaid in the nearby Finn's Hotel.

A LIVELY AIR, GRACEFUL CARRIAGE AND LONG AUBURN TRESSES — ah!

I MISTOOK HIM FOR A SWEDISH SAILOR – HIS ELECTRIC BLUE EYES, YACHTING CAP AND PLIMSOLLS. BUT WHEN HE SPOKE, WELL THEN, I KNEW HIM AT ONCE FOR JUST ANOTHER DUBLIN JACKEEN CHATTING UP A COUNTRY GIRL.

Nora lost interest and failed to keep the appointment she'd made to meet him later in the week.

16 June 1904

Doggedly persistent, Joyce finally persuaded her to meet him on June 16th. She and James went walking on a beach in the inner suburbs of Dublin near Sandymount. It seems likely that some simple form of sexual intimacy took place between them. This hallowed the day for Joyce.

Elopement

They were young, they had no money, parental approval was not sought or given on either side. There was no formal engagement, indeed no legal marriage, but within a few months they had eloped to Europe.

They were unable to buy each other anything, apart from the bare necessities for their voyage. But, years later, Joyce was to give Nora the greatest gift – the memory of 16 June 1904 – that single day in which the entire action of **Ulysses** takes place, immortalized in that novel.

James and Nora – an apparently ill-matched pair – the brilliant intellectual and the unlettered chambermaid. Joyce's father could not resist commenting on Nora's name.

And stick to him she did. They turned out ideal lifelong companions. To balance Joyce's cerebral gifts, Nora had a natural graciousness and wit. He was air and fire – she earth and water.

1904 was indeed a momentous year for Joyce. On January 17th, he sat down and wrote in one day an autobiographical sketch, "A Portrait of the Artist". Crude but original, it was the germ he later expanded into the unpublished **Stephen Hero**, and ultimately into **A Portrait of the Artist as a Young Man**. He submitted it to the magazine **Dana**.

Joyce also submitted three stories to (of all things!) an agricultural paper, **The Irish Homestead**, edited by the poet, theosophist and painter, George Russell. These were the kernel of his first prose work, **Dubliners**, and he signed them **Stephen Daedalus**!

The Martello Tower

Joyce had become friendly with a young medical student, Oliver St. John Gogarty, who was to be the model for Buck Mulligan in **Ulysses**. Gogarty was a poet and a noted athlete. Joyce was attracted by his irreverence, although he also suspected him.

HIS MUCH-VAUNTED BOHEMIANISM METHINKS DISGUISES A COLLABORATOR WITH THE DUBLIN LITERARY AND POLITICAL ESTABLISHMENT!

For a few days in early September 1904, Joyce stayed with him in the Martello Tower in Sandycove. These towers, 15 of which dotted the Irish coastline, were built in the early 1800s by the British as a defence against an anticipated Napoleonic invasion.

Gogarty rented the tower as a kind of bohemian nucleus.

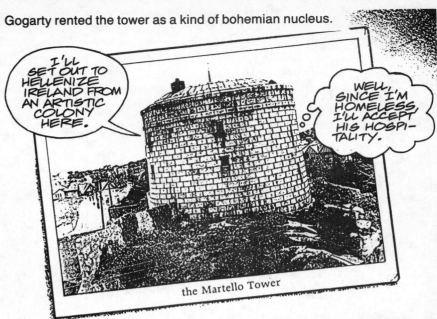

the Martello Tower

Relations between the two men were uneasy from the start.

The third member of the group was a highly strung Anglo-Irish man, Samuel Chenevix Trench, who ostentatiously spoke Irish and affected the Gaelic christian name "Dermot". He suffered from nightmares. On the night of 14 September, he dreamt of being chased by a black panther. Half asleep, he reached for the loaded revolver he kept by his side and shot into the fireplace, narrowly missing Joyce.

When he woke again, screaming about the panther, Gogarty took the gun from him and shouted, "Leave him to me!"

Joyce took this as notice to quit, got dressed and left, although it was the middle of the night. This incident provided the setting and atmosphere for the opening chapter of **Ulysses**.

Joyce and Nora left Ireland at the beginning of October 1904 and arrived in Zurich. Expectations of finding a teaching post for him in the Berlitz School were disappointed. The young couple were redirected to Austria, where they eventually settled down, first in Pola, and after a few months in Trieste, then an important naval port of the Austro-Hungarian Empire.

By the end of 1905, Joyce had completed **Chamber Music** (a volume of verse), **Dubliners** in its original form, and had written 500 pages of **Stephen Hero** (the original first draft of **A Portrait of the Artist as a Young Man**).

On 15 October 1905, Joyce contacted the London publisher, Grant Richards, offering him the manuscript of **Dubliners**. *"People might be willing to pay for the special odour of corruption which I hope floats over my stories."*

Richards was initially enthusiastic, but the printer rebelled at being asked to print stories he considered indecent, like "Two Gallants", and containing the word "bloody" for which he had a special aversion.

Oh, one eyed printer! Why has he descended with his blue pencil, full of the Holy Ghost, upon these passages and allowed his companions to set up in type reports of divorce cases and ragging cases and cases of criminal assault?

For nearly ten years, Joyce fought a lonely indomitable battle against prudish printers and prim publishers.

Barely 24 years of age, and with nothing under his belt save for a few undergraduate fragments, he had the *chutzpah* to tell Grant Richards: "It is not my fault that the odour of ash pits and old offal hangs around my stories. I seriously believe that you will retard the course of civilization in Ireland by preventing the Irish people from having one good look at themselves in my nicely polished looking glass."

Bravado or defence mechanism – the same is found when Joyce first met the established poet, W.B. Yeats, to whom he said on leaving, "I am twenty, how old are you?"

Yeats was offended and told his friends, "Such a colossal self-conceit with such a Lilliputian literary genius I never saw combined in one person."

The Joyces by now had two children, Giorgio, born July 1905, and Lucia, born the same month in 1907. In September 1909, Joyce returned to Dublin on a visit and managed to win a contract for **Dubliners** from the publisher, Maunsel & Company.

Joyce convened a group of Triestine businessmen, who had already successfully opened cinemas in Trieste and Bucharest, and unfolded his scheme.

I KNOW OF A CITY IN EUROPE WITH HALF A MILLION INHABITANTS IN WHICH THERE IS NOT ONE CINEMA.

AH, WHERE IS THAT?

I'LL TELL YOU, BUT ONLY IF YOU AGREE TO MY PLAN AND MAKE ME A PARTNER.

Joyce arrived back in Ireland on 21 October 1909, secured a building in Mary Street in the heart of Dublin, and set about remodelling it and hiring staff. Among those whose services he engaged was a projectionist, Lennie Collinge, who as an old man told the present writer: "Ah poor Mr Joyce. He was a gentleman all right. But he wasn't able for the electricians. They ran rings around him."

The cinema was named the **Volta** and opened its doors on 20 December, in time for the Christmas rush.

Cinematic Joyce

Although his professional connection with the Volta was not to last, Joyce maintained an interest in the world of film. Some of his later techniques, like the use of flashback in **A Portrait of the Artist as a Young Man**, and the dissolving of one scene into another in **Finnegans Wake**, probably derive from his understanding of early cinema.

Much later he was to discuss with the Russian director, Sergei Eisenstein, the possibility of filming **Ulysses**, and even helped some friends to prepare an outline scenario for the filming of the "Anna Livia Plurabelle" episode of **Finnegans Wake**.

Despite the apparent triumph of the Volta opening, Joyce was now confronted with irate landlords threatening to evict both the Dublin and Trieste branches of the family simultaneously for non-payment of rent. Returning to Trieste in January 1910, Joyce found himself embroiled again with publishers, landlords and an increasingly rebellious family.

"Oh joking Jesus! Here it is July and Maunsel are postponing DUBLINERS yet again!"

OGRAPHE PERFECTI
YSTEME JOLY)

Nora Joyce, who had become homesick, left with Lucia in July 1912 for a visit to her mother in Galway. Within a week, Joyce followed them and was soon engaged once more in tortuous negotiations with the representative of Maunsel & Company, George Roberts, over the publication of **Dubliners**. Despite Joyce's most ingenious efforts, Roberts became more and more intractable.

Joyce offered his one proof copy to various publishers, including the firm of Mills and Boon (!), on his way through London to Trieste.

Sick at heart, Joyce spent the train journey composing a savage satire against publishers and all they represent.

Look now, every and any kind of vulgarity or indecency is tolerable in real life, so long as it's not put into print. You can say that a book of verse "would give heartburn on your arse", or to exclaim under duress, "Shite and onions!", but you've no right to print the word "bloody" or the names of the Wellington Monument or Sydney Parade or the Sandymount tram, as these are too ordinary for notice by the artist.

Two more years passed before Joyce managed to get Grant Richards to publish **Dubliners** (with only very marginal changes). That was in June 1914.

Dubliners and "Scrupulous Meanness"

"I do not think that any writer has yet presented Dublin to the world."
Joyce

Most volumes of short stories are collections or anthologies from various sources. **Dubliners** is unusual in being conceived from the start as a book in itself, with stories linked together by theme, style, technique and subject matter. In a letter of 5 May 1906 to Grant Richards, Joyce writes: "My intention was to write a chapter of the moral history of my country and I chose Dublin for the scene because that city seemed to be the centre of paralysis. I have tried to present it to the indifferent public under four of its aspects: childhood, adolescence, maturity and public life. The stories are arranged in this order. I have written it for the most part in a style of **scrupulous meanness** . . ."

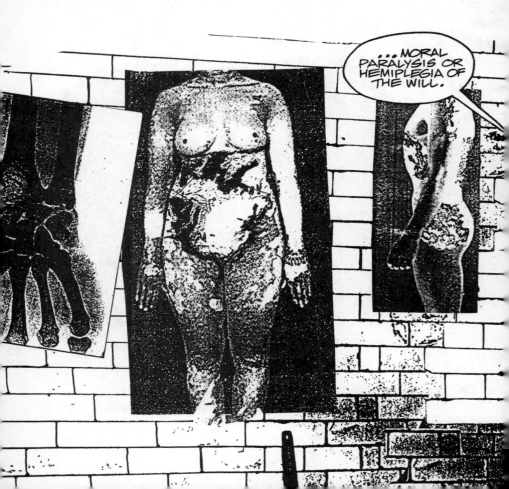

Stanislaus Joyce noted in his diary during the composition of the early stories: "He (J.J.) talks much of the syphilitic contagion in Europe, is at present writing a series of studies of it in Dublin, tracing practically everything to it."

Many years later, when Georges Goyert proposed translating **Dubliners** into French under the title, **How They Are in Dublin**, Joyce rebuked him sharply.

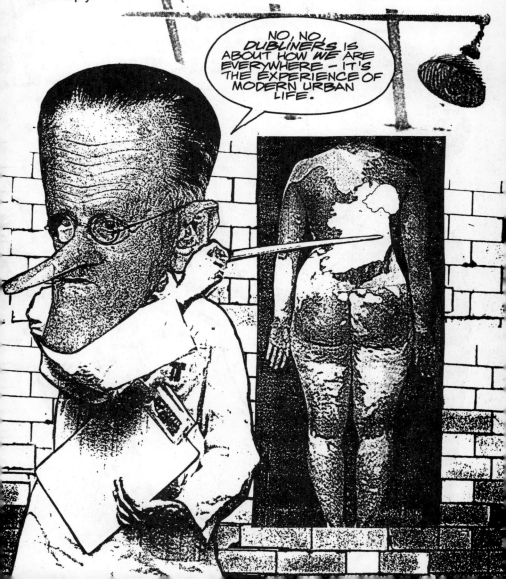

A Restricted Palette – but a Comprehensive Picture

"Scrupulous meanness" is a striking and very precise phrase. What did Joyce mean by it?

Joyce, who had an extraordinary command over language, deliberately limited his vocabulary in **Dubliners**. This is partly to give a sense of the niggardly quality of the lives lived by his characters. A good example of this would be the landlady or "Madame", Mrs Mooney, in the story "The Boarding House".

Joyce deploys a concentrated vocabulary in which words like "vain", "useless", "tiresome", "hopeless" etc., recur from story to story. The effect of this is to sensitize the reader subliminally to the moral texture of each story.

Another key word is "confused". Even where it does not appear, the confusion itself invariably does as an indicator of paralysis. Characters become confused and immobilized like frightened rabbits whenever they have to confront the risk of choosing a positive life.

Joyce's almost monochrome prose surface – like the dull Dublin climate – ends by producing the effect of sepia-toned period photographs. But these stories are no mere nostalgic snapshots of Edwardian Dublin.

The action of the stories is minimal, and the characters are seen as victims of a system that breeds paralysis. At the end of a story, the reader should view its slight events with eyes subtly changed by the process itself of reading that story.

All this might suggest that **Dubliners** is a rather bleak and forbidding book – or even boring. No doubt, Joyce deliberately sabotages the reader's normal expectations of stories with a "beginning, a middle and an end". Joyce's stories do not rely on any flashy "twist" in the plot, but a subtle turning-point which lingers in one's memory.

Let's examine a story from **Dubliners**, "The Sisters".

The Sisters

It is 1895. An unnamed boy – perhaps 13 years of age, as Joyce himself would then have been – passes the house of a priest, Father James Flynn, dying of paralysis. The priest has been his mentor, and every night the boy looks out for the candlelight at the window that will signal the paralytic's death. He repeats the word "paralysis" to himself.

"Paralysis" fills him with dread, but he wishes "to look on its deadly work".

Sometime later, at supper in the house of his uncle and aunt, he finds a family friend, Old Cotter, talking of Fr Flynn. Like most of the adults in the story, Old Cotter leaves his sentences hanging unfinished in the air.

The boy used to be interested in Old Cotter's knowledge of "faints" and "worms", technical terms of distilling, but he had been replaced by Fr Flynn's more fascinating information on the "mysteries of the Church".

The boy's uncle says that Fr Flynn has just died.

The boy has difficulty in sleeping as he puzzles angrily over Old Cotter's unfinished sentences. He imagines seeing the grey face of the paralytic and tries to exorcize it by thinking of Christmas. But the priest's face pursues him in the dark, smiling, and with "spittle-moist" lips murmurs a confession, to which the boy responds with a feeble smile of absolution.

Next day, 1 July 1895, he goes to the dead priest's house – a drapery shop, closed, with a crêpe bouquet on the door knocker. He remembers past visits to Fr Flynn – the gift packets of High Toast snuff he brought from his aunt.

Now the boy recalls what Fr Flynn taught him – to pronounce Latin correctly, stories of the catacombs and Napoleon Bonaparte, and the meaning of the ceremonies and vestments used at Mass.

HE SHOWED ME HOW COMPLEX AND MYSTERIOUS WERE THE INSTITUTIONS OF THE CHURCH.

That evening, the boy returns with his aunt to visit the dead priest. One of Fr Flynn's sisters, Nannie, escorts them upstairs to the dead room.

Would he find the dead priest smiling, as in his dream?

But, no . . . he was not smiling. There he lay, solemn and copious, vested as for the altar, his large hands loosely retaining a chalice . . . There was a heavy odour in the room – the flowers.

They join the other sister Eliza downstairs and are served sherry. The boy's aunt delicately probes Eliza about the death.

What originally provoked Fr Flynn's strange imbalance of mind is only partly resolved by Eliza.

The story ends here, left hanging in the air.

Joining up the dots...

What is the story about? It must be interpreted from little clues, as the boy himself must do. The key is contained in the first choice of words, **paralysis**, **gnomon** and **simony**. Gnomon can refer to the sundial's index, but more simply means "one who knows" or "interpreter". Simony is the sinful attempt to buy the powers of the Holy Spirit. If the boy is the "interpreter", what then is the priest's sinful act of "simony"?

But first – why call the story "The Sisters"? After all, they do nothing of any great consequence, except for Eliza's commentary on the circumstances of their brother's paralysis and death. It is clear from Eliza's speech that they are from a lower-class poor background. In such families, it was socially advantageous to have a boy a priest, regardless of whether he had any real religious vocation. The sisters exist only in reference to their brother's position, from which they gain their social status.

But James Flynn can only understand religion in terms of rule books, dogma, vestments and ceremonials, and to function at all must cling to literal fundamentalist values. Thus, when he drops the chalice which contains the Real Presence of Christ, his reaction must be one of terror. To such a mind as his, the spilling of the chalice should have been accompanied by the Voice of God in anger. But nothing happened. The world just went on regardless. This silence of the godhead broke James Flynn's mind.

None of this is dishonourable or smacks of paralysis. What does indicate **simony** is the priest's retreat from any real understanding of his experience into perversity by returning to rule book answers in which he no longer believes, tomes as thick as the telephone directory which puzzle and confuse the innocent young boy. He commits simony by clinging to the **material** equivalence of the spirit.

Joyce's method is really modern. The story he presents is incomplete on the page. It requires the active participation of the reader for its fulfilment.

Joyce gave a name to this gradual revelation of a story's inner core of meaning. He called it an "epiphany". His terminology is religious, referring to the Epiphany of Christ, when the infant God King was displayed to the Three Wise Men.

An example of an epiphany occurs in **Stephen Hero**, as Stephen Dedalus strolls down Eccles Street on a misty evening and overhears a conversation.

A young lady was standing on the steps of one of those brown brick houses which seem the very incarnation of Irish paralysis. A young gentleman was leaning on the rusty railings of the area...

THE YOUNG LADY – (drawling discreetly)...Oh, yes...I was... at the...cha...pel...

THE YOUNG MAN – (inaudibly)...I...(again inaudibly)...I...

THE YOUNG LADY – (softly)...Oh...but you're...ve...ry... wick...ed...

The triviality made him think of collecting many such moments together in a book of epiphanies. By an epiphany he meant a **sudden** spiritual manifestation, *whether in the vulgarity of speech or of gesture or in a memorable phase of the mind itself.*

For Joyce. the artist is like a priest who transmutes ordinary bread and wine into the Body and Blood of Christ.

A Portrait of an Artist as a Young Man

Joyce's great novel, **A Portrait of the Artist as a Young Man**, was published on 29 December 1916. The novel is composed of five chapters which trace the development of its central character, Stephen Dedalus.

Stephen's experiences are by and large the unheroic, commonplace ones of humanity in general. What sets him apart from his peers is the single-minded integrity and searing honesty of his response to these experiences, whether they be wetting the bed as a child, finding his way towards sexual identity as an adolescent, or writing self-indulgent poetry as a young man. Most significantly, Joyce demonstrates how an individual conscience can be formed and can create its own system of values, independent of the prevailing hypocrisy and half-truths of society.

The title clearly parallels the artist's self-portrait, a tradition from Rembrandt to Van Gogh, but it is a **young man**'s portrait – Joyce himself drawing on his own youthful Dublin experiences. However, this is art and not simply autobiography.

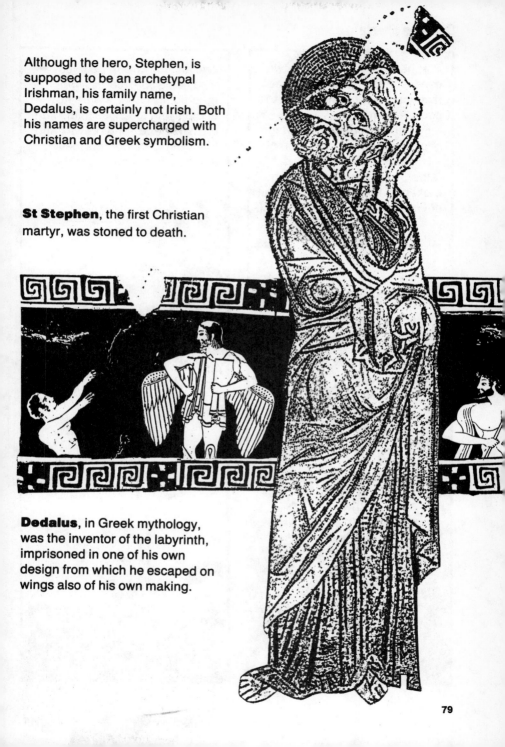

Although the hero, Stephen, is supposed to be an archetypal Irishman, his family name, Dedalus, is certainly not Irish. Both his names are supercharged with Christian and Greek symbolism.

St Stephen, the first Christian martyr, was stoned to death.

Dedalus, in Greek mythology, was the inventor of the labyrinth, imprisoned in one of his own design from which he escaped on wings also of his own making.

Double Dedalus

Stephen is a "Dedalus" in two senses. First, like Dedalus the mythical inventor, he strives to escape from the narrow labyrinth of Dublin life on wings of art. Second, he is the son of a Dedalus – Simon Dedalus, his father, whose inventive tongue makes an imprisoning maze out of family life.

The ancient Greek Dedalus also had a son, Icarus, who ignored his father's warning about flying too close to the sun on man-made wings of wax and feathers. Icarus' wings melted and he plummeted to his death in the sea.

PLOP

Joyce underlines the links – the artist Dedalus; escape from Ireland; over-reaching Icarus – by a motto from the Roman poet Ovid in his Book 8 of **The Metamorphoses** which prefaces the novel – *Et ignotas animum dimittit in artes* – "he sent his mind searching after hidden knowledge".

Stephen's search for hidden, forbidden knowledge is a constant theme reinforced by parallels to the mythic Prometheus, the titan who stole fire from the gods, punished by being chained to a rock and having his liver eaten by vultures – suggested in the scene from Stephen's infancy.

Another Icarus parallel is Lucifer (the "light-bearer") whose defiant cry – **non serviam**, "I will not serve" – is echoed by Stephen.

Time and again, Joyce's prose consciously imitates the swooping sunward flight of Icarus, only to come down to earth with a thud. One of many such "up/down" examples occurs at the end of chapter 2, a description of Stephen's first sexual experience with a prostitute which peaks on a note of ecstatic abandon.

Stephen's "high" does not last, and we find him in the next chapter plunged in the trough of delayed post-coital melancholy, as he contemplates a dull December day through the school-room window and he feels his belly "crave for its food".

> He hoped there would be stew for dinner, turnips and carrots and bruised potatoes and fat mutton pieces to be ladled out in thick peppered, flour-fattened sauce. Stuff it into you, his belly counselled him.

Let's now look at some central features of the 5 chapters in sequence.

Chapter 1: from Embryo

The novel opens with the "embryonic" prattling of baby Stephen in the nursery.

...and this moocow that was coming down along the road met a nicens little boy named baby tuckoo...

All five senses are represented in the first two introductory pages.

hearing × *"his father told him that story"*

sight × *"his father looked at him through a glass"*

taste × *"she sold lemon platt" (a sticky sweet)*

touch × *"When you wet the bed, first it is warm. Then it gets cold"*

smell × *"his mother put on the oil sheet. That had the queer smell"*

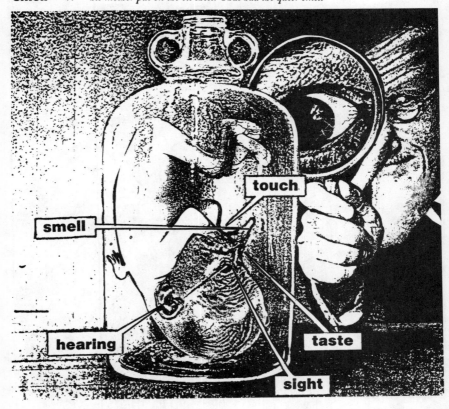

All the major themes of the book are also found symbolized in the first pages, including politics, represented by (aunt) Dante's brushes – the "maroon velvet back" for Michael Davitt and the "green velvet back" for Parnell.

If the nursery "moocow" is a lyrical up-swoop, the down-to-earth thump is then found early in chapter 2 when Stephen encounters the offending truth of real cows.

...the first sight of the filthy cow yard at Stradbrook with its foul green puddles and clots of liquid dung and steaming brantroughs sickened Stephen's heart. The cattle which had seemed so beautiful in the country on sunny days revolted him...

Chapter 2: School Days

Early infancy is over in two pages. A gap of several years follows before we land in the school playing-fields of Clongowes. Joyce is not concerned with strict linear day-by-day time, but with psychological development. A change in language conveys Stephen's new experience, as Joyce deftly captures the language of the school yard. *"Rody Kickham was a decent fellow but nasty Roche was a stink."*

Stephen, out in the cold of the rugby field, would prefer to be snug indoors. He meditates on some sentences in a spelling book.

It would be nice to lie on the hearthrug before the fire, leaning his head upon his hands, and think on those sentences. He shivered as if he had cold slimy water next his skin. That was mean of Wells to shoulder him into the square ditch because he would not swap his little snuffbox for Wells's seasoned hacking chestnut, the conqueror of forty. How cold and slimy the water had been! A fellow had once seen a big rat jump into the scum. Mother was sitting at the fire with Dante waiting for Bridget to bring in the tea. She had her feet on the fender and her jewelly slippers were so hot and they had such a lovely warm smell!

Note how the words divide into appropriate groupings – "nice, hearthrug, fire, mother, tea"etc., as against "shivered, cold slimy water, mean, rat, scum" etc. Stephen measures words and sounds against the reality they reflect: *"By thinking about things you could understand them."*

And the Shadow of Parnell . . .

In a Christmas dinner scene, Joyce captures the terrifying energies released by the Parnellite split, when the Irish party divided on the issue of whether Parnell as an adulterer was morally fit to be leader. A guest at dinner, Mr Casey, tells a story of spitting his tobacco juice at an old harridan, one of the hecklers in an anti-Parnell mob at a meeting.

Dante reacts in fury with the slogan . . .

Dante leaves the table and shouts back violently

DEVIL OUT OF HELL! WE WON! WE CRUSHED HIM TO DEATH! FIEND!

Mr Casey sobs loudly and bitterly.

POOR PARNELL! MY DEAD KING!

Terror-stricken Stephen sees his father's eyes full of tears.

Chapter 3: Repentance

Chapter 3 focuses almost entirely on a three-day religious retreat at Belvedere College in Stephen's adolescence. Although this penitential form of "self-examination" is deeply Catholic, it can bring a shudder to anyone familiar with the childhood terrors of Protestant, Islamic, Jewish or political fundamentalism.

Father Arnall, who leads the retreat, preaches a series of chilling hell-fire sermons.

The very air of this world, that pure element, becomes foul and unbreathable when it has been long enclosed. Consider then what must be the foulness of the air of hell. Imagine some foul and putrid corpse that has lain rotting and decomposing in the grave, a jellylike mass of liquid corruption. Imagine such a corpse a prey to flames, devoured by the fire of burning brimstone and giving off dense choking fumes of nauseous loathsome decomposition. And then imagine this sickening stench, multiplied a millionfold and a million fold again from the millions upon millions of fetid carcasses massed together in the reeking darkness, a huge and rotting human fungus. Imagine all this and you will have some idea of the horror of the stench of hell.

Stomach churning with fear and guilt, Stephen staggers to the Church Street Chapel and makes his confession.

After confession, Stephen's prayers *"ascended to heaven from his purified heart like perfume steaming upwards from a heart of white rose."*

Life seems simple and sanctified once more. Even the poor kitchen at home looks touched by heavenly grace.

Chapter 4: Rejecting the Priesthood

At the start of chapter 4, religious ecstasy has already descended into a rigmarole of meaningless routine devotions.

Sunday was dedicated to the mystery of the Holy Trinity, Monday to the Holy Ghost, Tuesday to the Guardian Angels, Wednesday to St. Joseph, Thursday to the Most Blessed Sacrament of the Altar, Friday to the Suffering Jesus, Saturday to the Blessed Virgin Mary.

Soon after, Stephen is summoned to a private meeting. The Jesuit Director of Belvedere asks Stephen to consider the possibility of a priestly vocation. It is a tempting offer of power to a boy of Stephen's shattered background.

Stephen knows himself tempted by the sin of simony (an echo of "The Sisters" story in **Dubliners**) – *"the sin against the Holy Ghost for which there was no forgiveness."*

Stephen rejects the Director's seductive offer. This is a major turning-point in the novel, but it is conveyed to us by discreet suggestion rather than by anything melodramatic.

As Stephen shakes hands with the old Director, a quartet of young men pass by singing. Their cheerfulness makes Stephen smile.

Stephen detaches his hand – and his fate – from the cheerless world of priests. Without explicitly stating anything, Joyce makes it clear that Stephen will never now become a priest.

Stephen has remained true to an artist's vocation. The chapter closes with his mystical encounter – a beautiful "bird-like girl" on the strand at Bull Island – which makes clear to him what his fate really is.

We are left with the quiet ecstasy of the Celtic twilight – an image of the moon reflected in sea pools.

With typical irony, Joyce turns this romantic vision of moonlit pools into a kitchen scene of breakfasting on "yellow drippings" of fat and fried bread at the start of chapter 5.

Chapter 5: the Shadow of Another's Language

At university, language is still central to Stephen's concerns, demonstrated in a simple incident.

Late for a lecture, Stephen bumps into the Dean of Studies, an English convert to Catholicism, who is lighting a coal fire in the grate. **Funnel** is the word the Dean uses in describing how oil is poured into a lamp.

This exchange over unfamiliar words prompts Stephen to reflect on the English language – which tells us much about Irish writers and Joyce in particular.

> The language in which we are speaking is his before it is mine. How different are the words *home*, *Christ*, *ale*, *master*, on his lips and on mine! I cannot speak or write these words without unrest of spirit. His language, so familiar and so foreign, will always be for me an acquired speech. I have not made or accepted its words. My voice holds them at bay. My soul frets in the shadow of his language.

Despite his courage and integrity, Stephen is still treated ironically by Joyce. The elaborate machinery of Stephen's aesthetic theories, borrowed wholesale from the medieval theologian St Thomas Aquinas, serves only to bring forth a second-rate poem.

Throughout the novel, the pressures on Stephen have been to "apologize, repent, submit, conform, confess". At last, as we come to the novel's resolution, Stephen makes his secular confession to his friend Cranly.

You made me confess the fears that I have. But I will tell you also what I do not fear. I do not fear to be alone or to be spurned for another or to leave whatever I have to leave. And I am not afraid to make a mistake, even a great mistake, a lifelong mistake and perhaps as long as eternity too.

A Portrait of the Artist ends in diary form, which is meant to represent the final detachment of Stephen's personality. (In his diary, Stephen records looking up the word "tundish" and finding that it is "good old blunt English".)

There is a final clarion call of youthful pride at the end as Stephen prepares to take flight from Dublin on Dedalus wings of art.

Welcome, oh life! I go to encounter for the millionth time the reality of experience and to forge in the smithy of my soul the uncreated conscience of my race.

But in the background, there is a very Irish figure, his mother, helping him to pack and praying wistfully.

MAY HE LEARN IN HIS OWN LIFE AND AWAY FROM HOME AND FRIENDS WHAT THE HEART IS AND WHAT IT FEELS.

And What the Critics Said...

When **A Portrait** was published in 1916, the response by most critics, unaware of the novel's systematic organization, was puzzlement.

It is very difficult to know quite what to say about this new book by Mr Joyce. **Literary World**

Mr Joyce is a clever novelist. but we feel he would be really at his best in a treatise on drains **Everyman**

But Joyce had powerful allies too, like the American poet Ezra Pound.

Joyce is a writer, GODDAMN your eyes. Joyce is a writer, I tell you, etc. etc. Lewis can paint, Gaudier knows a stone from a milk pudding. WIPE your feet!!!!

In March 1914, Joyce began serious work on his next great novel, **Ulysses**, but put it aside to write his one (unsuccessful) play, **Exiles**, finished in 1915. The same year, he left for neutral Switzerland to avoid the First World War.

Eyes, Apologize...

After the war, Joyce returned for a few months to Trieste, where several episodes of **Ulysses** were completed, but ultimately settled in Paris in June 1920. France was to be the Joyces' home until shortly before James' death in 1941.

From 1917, Joyce's eyesight deteriorated, and during the last 20 years of his life he endured eleven painful eye operations. In the 1920s, while writing **Finnegans Wake**, he was almost completely blind at times and dosed with the drug Scopalomine.

There's a cough mixture Scopalomine,
And its equal has never been seen
'Twould make staid Tutankamen
Laugh and leap like a salmon
And his mummy hop scotch on the green.

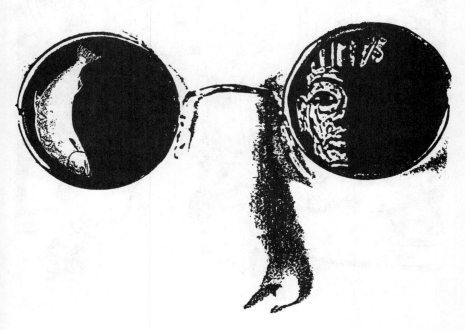

Financial Rescue

Although 1917 was a bad year for Joyce's eyes, it was also lucky, for in this year a remarkable English Quaker woman, Harriet Weaver, began to support him financially, and continued to do so with unwavering generosity until his death.

A Key Masterpiece of 20th Century Modernism

We can turn to Joyce's letter to the Italian critic, Carlo Linati, for an outline of his intention in writing **Ulysses**.

It is an epic of two races (Israelite-Irish) and at the same time the cycle of the human body as well as a little story of a day (life). The character of 'Ulysses' always fascinated me – even when a boy. Imagine, 15 years ago I started writing it as a short story for 'Dubliners'! For 7 years I have been working at this book – blast it! It is also a sort of encyclopedia. My intention is to transpose the myth *sub specie temporis nostri*. Each adventure (that is, every hour, every organ, every art being interconnected and interrelated in the structural scheme of the whole) should not only condition but even create its own technique. Each adventure is so to say one person although it is composed of persons – as Aquinas relates of the angelic hosts. No English printer wanted to print a word of it. In America the review was suppressed four times. Now, as I hear, a great movement is being prepared against the publication, initiated by puritans, English Imperialists, Irish Republicans, Catholics – what an alliance! Gosh I ought to be given the Nobel Prize for peace.

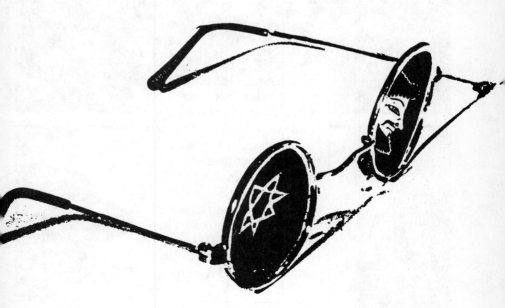

A 3-Dimensional Figure

What attracted Joyce to the Greek epic hero, Ulysses? He explained this in a conversation with Frank Budgen. Joyce challenged Budgen to name a writer who had produced the most all-round character in world literature.

No-age Faust isn't a man. But you mentioned Hamlet. Hamlet is a human being, but he is a son only. Ulysses is son to Laertes, but he is father to Telemachus, husband to Penelope, lover of Calypso, companion in arms of the Greek warriors around Troy and King of Ithaca. He was subjected to many trials, but with wisdom and courage came through them all.

Homer's Odyssey

To enjoy Joyce's **Ulysses**, the reader does not need a profound scholarly knowledge of Homer's epic, **The Odyssey** (the original Greek title, describing the wanderings of the hero Odysseus, Latinized as Ulysses). An acquaintance with Homer's epic will certainly sharpen one's appreciation of Joyce's modern version, and it is essential to be at least familiar with an outline of Homer's original.

What is the story of Odysseus as told by Homer (circa 750 B.C.)?

Odysseus was one of the Greek heroes who besieged and finally captured the city of Troy, a revenge for the adulterous elopement of Helen, wife of King Menelaus, with Paris, prince of Troy.

Odysseus suffered 10 years' delay in returning home to Ithaca, his punishment for having offended the sea god Poseidon. Thanks to his renowned cunning, Odysseus survived all the detours and perilous adventures that Poseidon inflicted on him. Odysseus encountered man-eating giants, the witch Circe who changed men into pigs, monsters, clashing rocks and whirlpools, and even travelled to the underworld of Hades to speak with the dead.

Meanwhile, at home, his wife Penelope who faithfully awaits his return, is being courted by 120 princes, each hoping to marry her and take the throne. The princes plot to murder Telemachus, son of Odysseus, when he returns from searching for his father.

Odysseus finally reaches home and in disguise kills all the suitors who have settled in his palace, drunk his wine, devoured his cattle and seduced his maid-servants.

Comic Translations

Joyce makes 1904 Dublin the adventurous geography through which his Odysseus/Ulysses wanders. Whom did Joyce choose to play the role of modern Ulysses? He cast an ordinary, mild salesman, Leopold Bloom, a Jewish "alien" to play the central role in a deeply Irish book. Bloom is the modern-day, comic, realist anti-hero "translation" of the epic hero Odysseus.

There are many other character "translations" paralleling Homer's original. Here are the three main characters.

DEDALVS

Stephen Dedalus (from **A Portrait**) parallels Telemachus, the son who goes in search of his wandering father Odysseus.

Stephen/Telemachus occupies the first 3 chapters of **Ulysses**, beginning with him in Buck Mulligan's (Gogarty's) Martello Tower.

"Roly poly" Leopold Bloom (Ulysses) is first introduced to us at home, cooking breakfast at 8 a.m.

Bloom's wife, Molly, parallels Odysseus' wife, patient Penelope faithfully awaiting the hero's return – except Molly isn't faithful and is having an affair with the rakish Blazes Boylan.

A useful map to orientate the reader

The schema below names the sections and chapters, based on Homer's **Odyssey**, which are untitled in Joyce's **Ulysses**. It supplies the Dublin locations, the hour-by-hour schedule and the symbolic themes Joyce develops.

TITLE	SCENE	HOUR	ORGAN	ART
I Telemachia				
1 Telemachus	: The Tower	: 8 am	:	theology
2 Nestor	: The School	: 10 am	:	history
3 Proteus	: The Strand	: 11 am	:	philology
II Odyssey				
1 Calypso	: The House	: 8 am	: kidney	:: economics
2 Lotuseaters	: The Bath	: 10 am	: genitals	: botany, chemistry
3 Hades	: The Graveyard	: 11 am	: heart	: religion
4 Eolus	: The Newspaper	: 12 noon	: lungs	: rhetoric
5 Lestrygonians	: The Lunch	: 1 pm	: esophagus	: architecture
6 Scylla and Carybdis	: The Library	: 2 pm	: brain	: literature
7 Wandering Rocks	: The Streets	: 3 pm	: blood	: mechanics
8 Sirens	: The Concert Room	: 4 pm	: ear	: music
9 Cyclops	: The Tavern	: 5 pm	: muscle	: politics
10 Nausikaa	: The Rocks	: 8 pm	: eye, nose	: painting
11 Oxen of Sun	: The Hospital	: 10 pm	: womb	: medicine
12 Circe	: The Brothel	: 12 midnight	: locomotor apparatus	: magic
III Nostos				
1 Eumeus	: The Shelter	: 1 am	: nerves	: navigation
2 Ithaca	: The House	: 2 am	: skeleton	: science
3 Penelope	: The Bed	: –	: flesh	: –

COLOUR	SYMBOL	TECHNIC	CORRESPONDENCES
: white gold	: heir	narrative (young)	(Stephen – Telemachus – Hamlet : Buck Mulligan – Antinous : Milkwoman – Mentor)
: brown	: horse	catechism (personal)	(Deasy : Nestor : Pisistratus : Sargent : Helen : Mrs O'Shea)
: green	: tide	monologue (male)	(Proteus – Primal Matter : Kevin Egan – Menelaus : Megapenthus : the Cocklepicker)
: orange	: nymph	narrative (mature)	(Calypso – The Nymph. Dlugacz : The Recall : Zion : Ithaca)
:	: eucharist	narcissism	(Lotuseaters : Cabhorses, Communicants, Soldiers, Eunuchs, Bathers, Watchers of Cricket)
: white black	: caretaker	incubism	(Dodder, Grand and Royal Canals, Liffey – The 4 Rivers : Cunningham – Sisyphus : Father Coffey – Cerberus : Caretaker – Hades : Daniel O'Connor – Hercules : Dignam – Elpenor : Parnell Aganemnon : Mentor : Ajax)
: red	: editor	enthymemic	(Crawford – Eolus : Incest – journalism : Floating Island – press)
:	: constables	peristalsis	(Antiphates – Hunger : The Decoy : Food : Lestrygonians : Teeth)
:	: Stratford, London	dialectic	(The Rock – Aristotle, Dogma, Stratford : The whirlpool : Plato, Mysticism, London Ulysses : Socrates, Jesus, Shakespeare)
:	: citizens	labyrinth	(Bosphorus – Liffey : European bank – Viceroy : Asiatic bank – Conmee : Symplegades Groups of citizens)
:	: barmaids	fuga per canonem	(Sirens – barmaids : Isle – bar)
:	: fenian	gigantism	(Noman – I : Stake – cigar : challenge – apotheosis)
: grey, blue	: virgin	tumescence detumescence	(Phaeacia – Star of the Sea : Gerty – Nausikaa)
: white	: mothers	embryonic development	(Hospital – Trinacria : Lampetie, Phaethusa – Nurses : Helios – Horne : Oxen – Fertility : Crime – Fraud)
:	: whore	hallucination	(Circe – Bella :)
:	: sailors	narrative (old)	(Eumeus – Skin the Goat : Sailor Ulysses Pseudangelos : Melanthius – Corly)
:	: comets	catechism (impersonal)	(Eurymachus – Boylan : Suitors – scruples : Bow – reason)
:	: earth	monologue (female)	(Penelope – Earth : Web – Movement)

Homer's Cyclops

Let's look at an episode in Homer, "The Cyclops", and then see how Joyce transforms it in **Ulysses**.

Odysseus and his crew land on an island inhabited by one-eyed giants called Cyclops. They are imprisoned in the cave of one of these giants, Polyphemus.

The Cyclops are cannibals and Polyphemus begins devouring the crew.

The wily Odysseus waits until one night Polyphemus is drunk on wine. Odysseus sharpens a stake, heats it in the fire and drives it into the giant's single eye, blinding him.

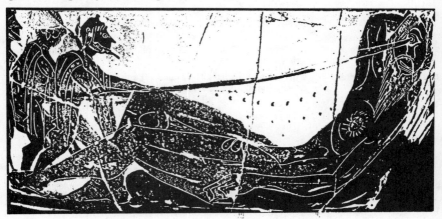

Odysseus had told Polyphemus that his name was **Outis** (no one). So when Polyphemus shouts that "No one is hurting me", the other giants ignore his cries, assuming him drunk.

In the morning, Polyphemus rolls away the boulder from the cave entrance to let his sheep out to graze. He feels their fleeces as they brush past him; but Odysseus and his men escape by clinging to the sheep's underbellies.

As they sail away from the island, Odysseus cannot resist shouting his real name back at the wounded giant pacing the shore. The sound gives Polyphemus a radar fix on the ship, and he flings a huge boulder at it, nearly causing a catastrophe.

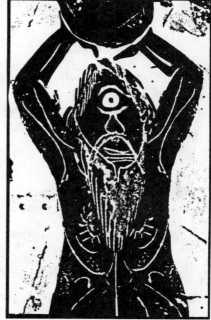

Joyce's Cyclops

"The Cyclops", chapter 9, opens with an absurdly-reduced version of the blinding of Polyphemus. "I was just passing the time of day with Old Troy of the D.M.P. at the corner of Arbour Hill there and bedamned but a bloody sweep came along and near drove his gear into my eye."

Barney Kiernan's pub becomes the Cyclop's cave, dominated by "the citizen", a British-hating Fenian nationalist whose foul-mouthed xenophobia parallels the one-eyed vision of Polyphemus. He and his companions are in a terrible (cannibalistic) state of thirst.

"One-eyedness" is conveyed by this single nameless "I" narrator of the chapter.

"Throwaway": A Chance Misunderstanding

Earlier in the day, Bloom had been accosted by Bantam Lyons who asked to see his paper for the racing form.

Bloom repeats what he's said, and Lyons answers, "I'll risk it."

Bloom (and we too) are puzzled by Lyon's cryptic reply at the time. But by 5 p.m., when unsuspecting Bloom enters Kiernan's pub, things have become clear, at least for us. On Thursday 16 June 1904, in fact and in fiction there was the Ascot Gold Cup horse race, and a total outsider called "Throwaway" romped home at 33 to 1. Bantam Lyons thinks Bloom has let slip a hot tip for the race.

The story has spread all over Dublin by the time Bloom enters the pub.

The barflies, who did not themselves have the courage to act on the "tip", assume Bloom has collected his winnings but is too mean to buy a round of drinks – although he does light up a cigar (shades of Odysseus' reddened stake!).

This releases the pent-up antagonism of the citizen and his cronies who taunt Bloom for his Jewishness. Bloom makes a brave stand against history.

The citizen (Polyphemus) throws, not a boulder, but a biscuit-box after Bloom who escapes on a jaunting-car. In a passage of comic pseudo-biblical prose, Bloom is transported into heaven like the prophet Elijah.

Like Odysseus, Bloom's imprudent revelation of his true identity nearly costs him a clout on the head!

Joyce is showing us that in our everyday lives we often unconsciously re-enact in miniature the essential themes of mythology.

Life Imitating Art

We have seen how a real horse race – the Ascot Gold Cup – is woven into the fiction of **Ulysses**. Let's consider two other events from Joyce's own life that overlap into **Ulysses**. The first incident helps explain why Joyce chose to make his Ulysses Jewish.

In the summer of 1904, a tipsy Joyce approached a young woman walking along Stephen's Green. Her boyfried took umbrage and fisticuffs ensued. Joyce was rescued by someone named Alfred Hunter. Mr Hunter had two things in common with the fictional Leopold Bloom – he was reputed to be Jewish and to have an unfaithful wife. Joyce toyed with the idea of a miniature Dublin odyssey for Mr Hunter as a story added to **Dubliners**.

No. 7 Eccles Street

Chapter 12, "Circe" or the brothel scene, ends with a drunk and confused Stephen Dedalus rescued by paternal Bloom (Mr Hunter) who takes him to 7 Eccles Street – Bloom's home and a real-life address of significance to Joyce.

During a visit Joyce made to Dublin in 1909, Vincent Cosgrave (the Lynch of **A Portrait**) told him a malicious story.

In despair, Joyce turned to an old friend J.F. Byrne (Cranly in **A Portrait**) who lived at 7 Eccles Street.

IT'S ALL PART OF A LOW PLOT BY GOGARTY AND HIS KIND WHO ARE JEALOUS OF YOUR GENIUS.

I'LL TELL YOU JIMMY WHAT COSGRAVE HIMSELF CONFESSED TO ME IN 1904 - THAT HE TRIED TO GET NORA FROM YOU BUT SHE SENT HIM MARCHING!

AH, SHE'S NOT UNFAITHFUL... BUT MY FRIENDS ARE!

Before leaving Dublin, Joyce called once more to thank Byrne. They went out walking, and upon their return Byrne discovered that he'd forgotten his latch key.

He vaulted over the railings, let himself down into the basement area and entered the house through the unlocked scullery door, and reappeared at the hall door to admit his companion...Stephen Dedalus.

This is precisely how Bloom lets Stephen into 7 Eccles Street in the "Eumeus" chapter of **Ulysses**.

Proteus: Intellectual Complexities

Perhaps the most intellectually complex episode is in section 1, chapter 3, "Proteus". Joyce scavenges the whole history of European scholastic philosophy to provide weapons for his young artist, Stephen Dedalus, in his battle to capture the transitory flux of reality.

Joyce relates this intellectual struggle to Homer's story of how King Menelaus wrestled information from the slippery old "shape-shifting" sea king, Proteus.

Bewildered by a myriad obscure references and complex patterns of language, ever shifting like the sea, the first-time reader may be tempted to give up.

A moment comes indeed when language seems to break down into meaningless misprinted shapes.

Listen: a four worded wave speech: seesoo, hrss, rsseeiss, ooos.

Do take Joyce's advice. Listen! For this is the miraculous moment when Stephen captures the voice of the sea itself in words of his own making – the crash of a wave and the foam retracted through the shingle.

Say it over to yourself. It is like putting a shell to your ear, as a child does to hear the sea.

Stream of Consciousness

Joyce perfected a **stream of consciousness** technique which imitates the way the mind "speaks" to itself – in complex fluid patterns, random interruptions, incomplete thoughts, half words and so on. Joyce claimed to have developed his technique from a forgotten French novel, **Les Lauriers sont coupés** by Edouard Dujardin, picked up in a railway kiosk.

Joyce strongly disagreed with those who believed that his stream of consciousness had been borrowed from Sigmund Freud's psychoanalytical theory of the unconscious.

Other writers at the time were developing similar ideas of the "inner mind". Virginia Woolf (1882–1941) describes a modernist practice of writing that fits Joyce's innovative technique in **Ulysses**.

Examine for a moment an ordinary mind on an ordinary day. The mind receives a myriad impressions – trivial fantastic evanescent, or engraved with the sharpness of steel. From all sides they come, an incessant shower of innumerable atoms; and as they fall, as they shape themselves into the life of Monday or Tuesday, the accent falls differently from of old . . . life is a luminous halo, a semi-transparent envelope surrounding us from the beginning of consciousness to the end. Is it not the task of the novelist to convey this varying, this unknown and uncircumscribed spirit, whatever abberation or complexity it may display, with as little mixture of the alien and external as possible?

An Example of Stream of Consciousness

Virtually all of **Ulysses** is written in this mode. Let's look at a typical example in chapter 5, "Lestrygonians". A glass of Burgundy wine and some Gorgonzola cheese that Bloom consumes in Davy Byrne's pub at 1 p.m. stirs up a memory of the day he first made love to Molly on Howth Head bay. The memory is framed by the sight of two flies copulating on the window.

Stuck on the pane two flies buzzed, stuck.

Glowing wine on his palate lingered swallowed. Crushing in the wine press grapes of Burgundy. Sun's heat it is. Seems to a secret touch telling me memory. Touched his sense moistened remembered. Hidden under wild ferns on Howth. Below us bay sleeping sky...

Ravished over her I lay, full lips full open, kissed her mouth. Yum. Softly she gave me in my mouth the seed cake warm and chewed. Mawkish pulp her mouth had mumbled sweet and sour with spittle. Joy: I ate it: joy. Young life, her lips that gave me pouting. Soft, warm, sticky, gumjelly lips, flowers her eyes were, take me, willing eyes. Pebbles fell . . .

Hot I tongued her. She kissed me, I was kissed. All yielding she tossed my hair, kissed, she kissed me.

Me. And me now.

Stuck, the flies buzzed.

The Sirens

Chapter 8, "Sirens", is dominated by the **ear** and **music**, and Bloom himself becomes a triumphantly comic musical instrument at the end. This is the effect on his guts of the Burgundy and Gorgonzola he had eaten at lunch. He feels a fart coming on, but he controls it as a lady passes near him. He pretends to study an illuminated text of Robert Emmet's **Speech from the Dock** in the window of a curio shop and waits for the noise of a passing tram to cover his embarrassment.

Seabloom, greasabloom viewed last words. Softly. *When my country takes her place among.*

Prrprr.

Must be the bur.

Fff. Oo. Rrpr.

Nations of the earth. No-one behind. She's passed. *Then and not till then.* Tram. Kran, kran, kran. Good oppor. Coming. Krandlkrankran. I'm sure it's the burgund. Yes. One, two. *Let my epitaph be.* Karaaaaaaa. *Written. I have.*

Pprrpffrrppfff.

Done.

Listening carefully to Joyce's musical effects helps us understand "Sirens", another difficult chapter like "Proteus". In it, Joyce is retelling Homer's story of the enchantress Sirens who sit on a rock and lure unwary sailors to certain death by their beautiful singing.

Odysseus is determined to be the one man to hear the sirens' song and survive. He commands his crew to stuff their ears against the sound and has himself lashed to the mast so that he cannot physically be drawn into the sirens' snare.

Bloom, at 4 p.m. in the Ormond Hotel, listens to Simon Dedalus singing the (enchanting) tenor air from the opera **Martha**. Bloom is aware that Blazes Boylan, Molly's lover, is about to leave the Ormond for his adulterous afternoon rendezvous with her. The last possible moment for Bloom's intervention passes as he listens to the aria . . . and he winds and unwinds an elastic band round his finger, binding himself to commonsense reality like his epic prototype, Odysseus.

The first 2 pages of "Sirens" is a baffling, apparently meaningless jumble of words. This is like an orchestra tuning up, in which we overhear little snatches of the melodies that are about to be played in full – a miniature rehearsal of everything we will "hear" in the chapter.

The 2-page rehearsal ends with two words: **done** (the last word which will end the chapter on Bloom's fart) and **begin!** (the only sound not heard again in the chapter) which is like the rap of a conductor's baton that "begins" the "full score" of the Sirens.

Other musical sound-effects abound. Bloom thinking of Molly's hair falling in tresses over her shoulders imitates a musical trill.

her wavyavyeavyheavyeavyevyevy hair un comb:, d.

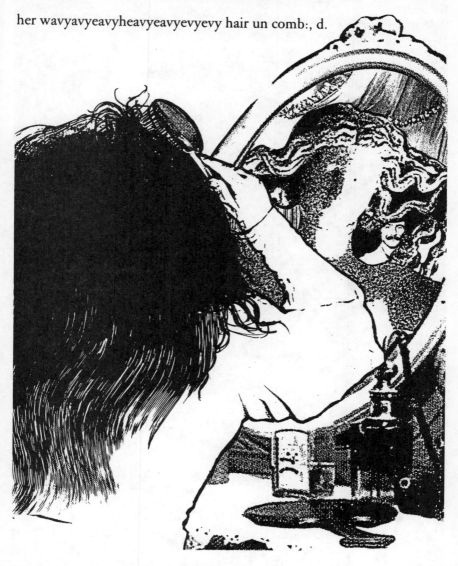

An arpeggio in music is made by leaving intervals (gaps) between the notes. Bloom standing up, in an accordion-like motion, is represented by an "arpeggio" phrase which leaves out the vowels, so that "Bloom stood up" becomes BLMSTDP.

Chapter 10: Nausikaa

Nausikaa in Homer is a lovely princess who assists the shipwrecked Odysseus – a moment of refreshment in his wanderings. Bloom's Nausikaa is Gerty McDowell, sitting on a rock on Sandymount Strand, who allows him a "refreshing" sight of her ankles – and his refreshment is masturbation.

Gerty's stream of consciousness is distilled from popular romantic pulp fiction which Joyce described in a letter to a friend as: *"a namby-pamby jammy marmalady drawersy (alto la!) style with effects of incense, mariolatry, masturbation, stewed cockles, painters palette, chit chat, circumslocution etc. etc."*

Bloom's peeping-Tom excitement, his erection and orgasm are filtered through Gerty's "marmalady" reveries as she watches an evening's fireworks display.

And then a rocket sprang and bang shot blind and o! Then the Roman candle burst and it was like a sigh of o! and everyone cried o! o! in raptures and it gushed out of it a stream of rain gold hair threads.

Only as Gerty limps away homeward does Bloom recognize that she is lame.

YES...

Just as Bloom gets momentary relief from Gerty, so too Molly enjoys brief satisfaction with Blazes Boylan. But at the end, in the "Penelope" chapter, Molly discards Boylan like a dildo, a "big red thing", and in her final stream of consciousness soliloquy she returns in her thoughts "faithfully" to Bloom as she slides off to sleep.

tomorrow the sun shines for you he said the day we were lying among the rhododendrons on Howth head in the grey tweed suit and his straw hat the day I got him to propose to me yes first I gave him the bit of seedcake out of my mouth and it was leapyear like now yes 16 years ago my God after that long kiss I near lost my breath yes he said I was a flower of the mountain yes so we are flowers all a womans body yes that was one true thing he said in his life and the sun shines for you today yes that was why I liked him because I saw he understood or felt what a woman is...

...then he asked me would I yes to say yes my mountain flower and first I put my arms around him yes and drew him down to me so he could feel my breasts all perfume yes and his heart was going like mad and yes I said yes I will Yes

The chapter – and the novel – end affirmatively with Molly's repeated **YES**. Beginning and end are joined in a circle – a perfect circle or not?

Resolution or Affirmation?

In comic novels – in Jane Austen's, for instance – we can expect that complications and misunderstanding always lead finally to harmony and resolution in marriage – the traditional "happy ending". Where is the resolution in **Ulysses**?

Stephen Dedalus, the Telemachus in search of a father, finds a surrogate in Bloom's paternal kindness – an encounter which occurs in a brothel and is in any case temporary, not a resolution.

Bloom is a married cuckold who releases his sexual tension by masturbating on Sandymount Strand, winding up at last upside-down in bed beside a wife with whom he has not had full sexual relations for nearly a dozen years. This too is hardly a conventionally resolved "happy ending". The resolution is a humanly **imperfect** circle.

It can be seen that Bloom and Molly share in an unorthodox form of communion. Throughout his day of journeying, Bloom's reveries remained anchored in Molly, and she at the end responds faithfully to him in her own thoughts. There is genuinely shared feeling, communion and reconciliation between them, far beyond the mechanical squirt of sperm.

Joyce is saying, life can be affirmed; it can never be absolutely resolved.

The Publication of Ulysses

In 1918, Margaret Anderson and Jane Heap began the serialization of **Ulysses** in New York in **The Little Review**. By October 1920 they had published about half the novel, when publication was terminated by an action for obscenity privately taken by the "New York Society for Suppression of Vice". The ban on **Ulysses** in the United States remained in force until 1933, when Judge John M. Woolsey gave his famous judgement: "a powerful commentary on the inner lives of men and women . . . I am quite aware that owing to some of its scenes **Ulysses** is a rather strong draught to ask some sensitive, though normal, persons to take. But my considered opinion, after long reflection, is that whilst in many places the effect of **Ulysses** on the reader undoubtedly is somewhat emetic, nowhere does it tend to be aphrodisiac. **Ulysses** may, therefore, be admitted into the United States." The week of the **Ulysses** decision saw also the repeal of Prohibition. As one door closed in 1920, another opened. This was the year, in Paris, that Joyce met Sylvia Beach, descendant of a long line of American Presbyterian ministers. She had opened a book shop, Shakespeare & Co., at 12 Rue de l'Odéon. In April 1921, she proposed publishing **Ulysses** in France, and Joyce agreed at once. **Ulysses** was published on his birthday, 2 February, 1922.

In Zurich, after a discussion about Irish wit and humour, Nora said to Joyce . . .

WHAT'S ALL THIS ABOUT IRISH WIT AND HUMOUR? HAVE WE ANY BOOK IN THE HOUSE WITH ANY OF IT IN? I'D LIKE TO READ A PAGE OR TWO.

Joyce was both irritated and amused by his wife's indifference to his genius. Though she never read **Ulysses**, it could not have been written without her. Not only is she the principal model for Molly Bloom (although she referred to her dismissively as a "horrible fat ugly married woman"), but it was under her influence and in exile that Joyce at last learnt as his mother had wished.

WHAT THE HEART IS AND HOW IT FEELS – A WISDOM I'VE PORTRAYED IN THAT DECENT ALL-ROUND MAN, LEOPOLD BLOOM.

Once **Ulysses** was safely launched, Joyce set to sifting through the mass of his notes left over from the writing of his novel for the seeds of his next work, **Finnegans Wake**. He was engaged on this book constantly for the next 17 years. At the same time, he also continued writing the delicate lyrical verse of his young manhood and, against the advice of the great modernist poet Ezra Pound, published them in **Pomes Penyeach** in 1927.

Sullivan's Champion

The same year, he became so disheartened by the almost universal opposition to **Finnegans Wake** that he considered abandoning it to his fellow Irishman, James Stephens, to finish. He also at this time developed a violently partisan admiration for the Irish tenor John Sullivan. Joyce felt that Sullivan had been frozen out by the operatic establishment just as he had earlier by the Dublin literary establishment. He was indefatigable in his pro-Sullivan propaganda and even organized a spectacular stunt during a performance of Rossini's **Guillaume Tell** at the Paris Opéra in which Sullivan appeared on 30 June 1930. As the newspapers reported it . . .

a sudden hush fell when a man in one of the boxes, whom many recognised as James Joyce, the Irish novelist and poet, dramatically leaned forward, raised a pair of heavy dark glasses from his eyes, and exclaimed: "Merci mon Dieu, pour ce miracle. Après vingt ans, je revois la lumière."*

(*Thank God for this miracle. After twenty years I see the light again.)

The Old Sinner Dies

Almost exactly a year later, John Stanislaus Joyce died in a Dublin hospital. Joyce was overcome by grief and guilt. He wrote with his usual penetrating insight about the role of his father in his life.

My father had an extraordinary affection for me. He was the silliest man I ever knew and yet cruelly shrewd. He thought and talked of me up to his last breath. I was very fond of him always, being a sinner myself, and even liked his faults. Hundreds of pages and scores of characters in my books came from him. His dry (or rather wet) wit and his expression of face convulsed me often with laughter. I got from him his portraits, a waistcoat, a good tenor voice, and an extravagant licentious disposition (out of which, however, the greater part of any talent I may have springs).

His Daughter's Breakdown

Joyce's birthday on 2 February 1932 was darkened by the unstable behaviour of his daughter Lucia who began to show pathological symptoms of schizophrenia. The famous Swiss analyst C.G. Jung examined Lucia.

YOU ARE LIKE TWO PEOPLE GOING TO THE BOTTOM OF A RIVER, BUT WHEREAS SHE IS DROWNING, YOU SIR ARE DIVING.

The clouds lifted a little with the birth of his grandson Stephen on 15 February 1932. Joyce wrote a simple but moving poem joining his father's death with the new arrival, **Ecce Puer** (Behold the Boy).

Of the dark past
a boy is born
With joy and grief
My heart is torn

Calm in his cradle
the living lies
May love and mercy
unclose his eyes!

Young life is breathed
upon the glass
The world that was not
Comes to pass

A child is sleeping:
An old man gone
Oh, Father forsaken,
Forgive your son!

As Lucia's illness worsened, Joyce still refused to give up hope. He fought despairingly but doggedly to save her, writing to Harriet Weaver in June 1936 that he would never lock her up in a "mental prison".

I will not do so as long as I see a single chance of hope for her recovery, nor blame her for the great crime she has committed in being a victim to one of the most elusive diseases known to men and unknown to medicine. And I imagine that if you were where she is and felt as she must you would perhaps feel some hope if you felt that you were neither abandoned nor forgotten.

Through all these difficulties and illnesses Joyce battled on with very little encouragement and amidst the growing threat of war to complete **Finnegans Wake** which was published on his 57th birthday, 2 February 1939. Joyce had kept the name of the book secret throughout its composition when it was published in sections as "work in progress".

Finnegans Wake

The great 18th century writer and lexicographer, Dr Samuel Johnson, said of another book by an Irishman, Lawrence Sterne's eccentric anti-novel **Tristram Shandy**, "Nothing so odd will last," and this was until recently a fairly common reaction to **Finnegans Wake**. Written between 1922 and 1939, it must have seemed very much part of the spirit of the age – the age of Picasso and jazz, Dali and Stravinsky, shattered perspective, melting watches and syncopated dissonances.

But there was a logic behind Joyce's curious production that showed him to be still a classicist at heart, always in control of the slightest detail of meaning and effect, even when painfully obscure to the reader.

The Book of the Night

In **Ulysses**, he had written his great book of the day and found in the "stream of consciousness" the key to the random associative patterns of the ordinary waking human mind. Now he set about piercing the secrets of the sleeping and the dead in his great night work **Finnegans Wake**.

To those who found it was too puzzling, he patiently replied . . .

They say it's obscure. They compare it with *Ulysses*. But the action of *Ulysses* was chiefly in the daytime. The action of my new work takes place at night. It's natural things should not be so clear at night, isn't it now?

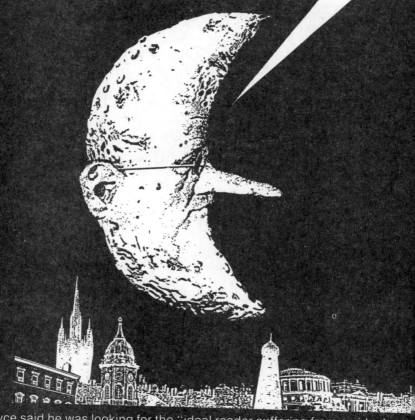

Joyce said he was looking for the "ideal reader suffering from an ideal insomnia".

What language is it written In?

At night in darkness (and remembering that Joyce was near blind at the time) the ear takes precedence over the eye. To those who found it unreadable, he suggested not reading but **listening** to it.

This is the reader's Golden Rule – **when in doubt, read aloud** – but try to do so with a Dublin accent.

Finnegans Wake is written in a night-time dream language. Its basic syntax and rhythm is that of Dublin-accented English, but there are echoes of almost **50 languages** from all over the world. Joyce sabotages our normal expectations of "daylight" commonsense language by using multi-level, multi-lingual puns which suggest many strata of meaning at the same time.

A (Blind) Irishman's Revenge

Joyce's revolutionary language is also to some degree a sophisticated linguistic revenge upon the English colonizers for 800 years of occupation. Joyce took over their most prized possession – the language of Milton and Shakespeare, smashed it into fragments and used the resulting "mess of mottage" to rewrite the history of the world.

No longer does his soul "fret in the shadow of another's language". Joyce makes one of his night-time characters Shem* boast that he would . . .

wipe alley English spooker multaphoniaksically spuking off the face of the erse . . .

(*The two sons of HCE and ALP are *Shem*, based on Joyce himself, and *Shaun*, his brother Stanislaus.)

The Tale of Sex

The universal history that Joyce offers us is at a fundamental level a simple story.

Joyce is saying what we all should know – that at the heart of every narrative is found romance, courtship and the sexual relationship (most frequently) between a man and a woman. Who are the man and the woman central to **Finnegans Wake**?

HCE and ALP

At a basic storyline level **Finnegans Wake** is the tale of the dream of a Dublin publican, Humphrey Chimpden Earwicker – HCE or Here Comes Everybody, the universal Everyman – and the woman is Anna Livia Plurabelle (ALP), HCE's wife. HCE, like other of Joyce's characters, echoes "the old reprobate", his father John Stanislaus Joyce.

How he used to hold his head as high as a howeth, the famous eld duke alien, with a hump of grandeur on him like a walking wiesel rat. And his derry's own drawl and his corksown blather and his doubling stutter and his gullaway swank.

The clue here is "high as a howeth". What is Joyce suggesting?

HCE broadens out beyond any one association and merges in a dream sense with Dublin itself. As he drifts off to sleep, we glimpse his form inset archeologically into the cityscape. We pass beneath the everyday contemporary surface down to deeper layers of Dublin's past – Victorian, Georgian, Elizabethan, Medieval and Viking. Gradually we recognize the outlines of a sleeping giant – his head formed by the Hill of Howth (Howth Head), arms extended in sleep around the bay, the trunk the city itself, the toes tucked up under the green sward of Castleknock, while from the bushes of the Phoenix Park there rises an enormous erection, "the Willingdone Mormorial Tallowscoop" (the Wellington Testimonial, an enormous obelisk erected to celebrate the Duke of Wellington's victories).

Just as HCE is not simply a man but collective humanity, a **male principle**, so also his wife Anna Livia Plurabelle becomes a **female principle** – Dublin's River Liffey (on old maps, the Liffey was called "Anna Liffey", from the Irish **amhain**, a river). ALP starts as a mere trickle in the Sallgap high up in the Dublin Mountains, makes her way merrily down the foothills, passes through the city and out into Dublin Bay where she merges with the sea, a kind of death, only to resurrect as a cloud which rains down the waters that will once more become a river, thus completing the circle.

Listen, you can hear the riverine music coursing through the prose...

slipping sly by Sallynoggin, as happy as the day is wet, babbling, bubbling, chattering to herself, deloothering the fields on their elbows leaning with a sloothering slide of her, giddy-gaddy, grannyma, gossipaceous Anna Livia.

He lifts the life wand and the dumb speak, Quoiquoiquoiquoiquoiquoiquoiq!

QUOI

QUOI

QUOI

QUOI

That last word is a wonderful Joycean touch. It is the voice of ducks born down on the bosom of the river. But they are educated French-speaking ducks quacking "what what what" as though in puzzlement at this strange book.

But why is it called Finnegans Wake?

Joyce took his title from an Irish-American ballad, "Finnegan's Wake", which tells of Tim Finnegan, the whisky-loving hod-carrier who fell from a ladder one day and cracked his skull. They took his corpse home for the traditional Irish merrymaking wake before the burial. The drink flows, a fight breaks out, and some whisky is spilt on Tim's corpse, with the result that he does indeed wake, exclaiming . . .

Tim Finnegan, a building labourer (Everyman or Adam) falling from a scaffold to his death only to be revived by spilt whisky (in Irish **uisce beatha**, water of life), fits in perfectly with Joyce's history of collective humanity's Fall, sleep, death and resurrection. This is a universal dream-history of **recurring archetypal figures** who merge the comic and the tragic – HCE and Finnegan = Adam and Humpty Dumpty = Mankind = Christ, Parnell, the blindness of Jonathan Swift, and so on.

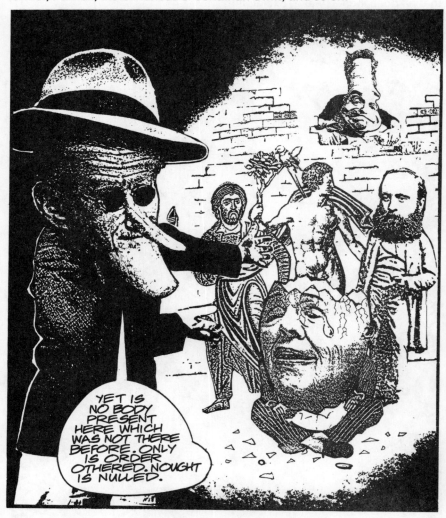

Joyce is saying, "Here Comes Everybody" – no one or nothing is lost, but the order (of appearance) is a different one.

The Perfect Circle

The structure of **Finnegans Wake** is circular, without beginning or end but constant rebirth. This cyclical idea is introduced at the beginning of the book with the second half of a sentence.

riverrun, past Eve and Adams, from swerve of shore to bend of bay, brings us by a commodius vicus of recirculation back to Howth Castle and Environs

Joyce has unspliced this part from its first half which he places at the **end** of the book.

The keys to. Given! A way, A lone, A last, A loved, A long the . . .

The reader has to splice them together again ("doublends jined") to grasp the circle of dreaming and waking that makes up human history.

Joyce is referring to an 8th century illuminated manuscript of the Gospels, famous for its exuberant Celtic decoration which almost obscures its initial capital letters. So too, the basic circular outline of **Finnegans Wake** is overlaid with elaborate tendrils of language.

Vico's Cycles of History

Let's look again at the truncated sentence which opens the book and focus on the words "commodius vicus of recirculation". This is an example of entangled Celtic design. **Commodius** refers to the Roman emperor Commodus, but also the etymological root of the word "commodious", meaning "convenient, roomy". **Vicus** is the Latin for village, and so the "roomy village" (of recirculation of history) is Dublin. And that's only the start of it!

Under the overload of historical puns, **vicus of recirculation** conjures up **Giambattista Vico** (1688 – 1744), Neapolitan philosopher of history.

Just as Joyce exploited Homer's epic in **Ulysses**, so here he borrows from Vico's theory of history. History for Vico consists of a series of cycles, the ebb and flow or "course and recourse" of ever-recurring epochs – The Divine Age, Heroic Age, Human Age followed by a period of chaos leading to the recommencing of the whole process once more. The beginning of this cycle in **Finnegans Wake** is heralded by a peal of thunder which recurs at intervals. On the very first page, we encounter the first of a series of hundred letter "thunderwords" –

Bababbadalgharaghtakamminarronnkonnbronntonnerronntuonnthunntrovarrhounawnskawntoohoohoordenenthurnuk!

A verbal oddity of this sort could make a reader give up. But we have to recognize that Joyce is actually imitating the sound of thunder here – its rolling clap and crescendo are marked by three unstressed syllables followed by a fourth stressed one: **bàbàbàdál.**

ALP in Brief

Perhaps the most easily approached section of **Finnegans Wake** is that known as "Anna Livia Plurabelle". This section was published separately as a slim volume by Faber & Faber in 1930. Joyce also chose to read the last pages of ALP for a live recording. Joyce described the chapter as "an attempt to subordinate words to the rhythm of water". He wrote to Miss Weaver that it was . . .

a chattering dialogue across the river by two washer women who, as night falls, become a tree and a stone. The river is named Anna Liffey. Some of the words at the beginning are hybrid Danish-English. Dublin is a city founded by Vikings. The Irish name is 'Baile Atha Cliath'. Ballyclee equals town or ford of hurdles. Her Pandora's box contains the ills flesh is heir to. The stream is quite brown, rich in salmon, very devious, shallow. The splitting up towards the end (seven dams) is the city abuilding.

Dirty Linen

Two washerwomen are overheard gossiping on the banks of the Liffey at Chapelizod on Dublin's outskirts, an ancient area associated with the legend of Tristan and Isolde, immortalized by Wagner's opera.

Appropriately for such a rivery episode, the first three lines form the shape of a delta.

O
tell me all about
Anna Livia! I want to hear all

One voice, dying to get the dirt on Anna Livia and her husband HCE, is constantly encouraging the other to garrulous disclosure of the sordid details: "Onon! Onon! tell me more. Tell me every tiny teign. I want to know every single ingul."

The pair discuss their clients' personal lives as they rinse out their intimate garments and make private linen public. They babble over the sinister significance of various stains – such as the recalcitrant one on HCE's underpants – and speculate on "whatever it was they tried to make out he tried to too in the fiendish park".

ALP too comes under the scrubbers' scrutiny, for, as they say in Dublin, "There's two of them in it."

The effect of their "gossipaceous" chatter is like overhearing snatches of argumentative conversation in a crowded restaurant.

The Hair of the River

Just as there is a remembrance of Joyce's father in HCE, so also he took hints from other real people to humanize the River Liffey. The waters of Anna Livia were reminiscent to Joyce of the long flowing hair of the wife of the writer Italo Svevo. Joyce remarked to an Italian journalist . . .

They say I have immortalised Svevo, but I have also immortalised the tresses of Signora Svevo. These were long and reddish blonde. My sister who used to see them let down told me about them. The river at Dublin passes dye-houses and so has reddish water. So I have playfully compared these two things in the book I am writing. A lady in it will have the tresses which are really Signora Svevo's.

Rumours about ALP abound, like soapsuds. At the time of her courtship she was just "a young thin pale soft shy slim slip of a thing." But even as a child, she escaped from parental control.

but first of all, worst of all, the wiggly livvly, she sideslipped out by a gap in the Devil's glen while Sally her nurse was sound asleep in a sloot and, feefee fiefie

She is said a gadabout from early on, even seducing some monkish hermits at Luggula.

Even when safely married, Dublin's river Anna Livia tarts herself up for a Saturday night date, sends an excuse to HCE and blithely sets out for an assignation.

First she let her hair fal and down it flussed to her feet its teviots winding coils. Then, mothernaked, she sampood herself with galawater and fraguant pistania mud, wupper and lauar, from crown to sole. Next she greesed the groove of her keel, warthes and wears and mole and itcher, with antifouling butterscatch and turfentide and serpenthyme and with leafmould she ushered round prunella isles and eslats dun, quincecunct, allover her little mary. Peeld gold of waxwork her jellybelly and her grains of incense anguille bronze. And after that she wove a garland for her hair. She pleated it. She plaited it. Of meadowgrass and riverflags, the bulrush and waterweed, and of fallen griefs of weeping willow. Then she made her bracelets and her anklets

and her armlets and a jetty amulet for necklace of clicking cobbles and
pattering pebbles and rumbledown rubble, richmond and rehr, of Irish
rhunerhinerstones and shellmarble bangles. That done, a dawk of smut
to her airy ey, Annushka Lutetiavitch Pufflovah, and the lellipos cream
to her lippeleens and the pick of the paintbox for her pommettes, from
strawbirry reds to extra violates, and she sendred her boudeloire maids
to His Affluence, Ciliegia Grande and Kirschie Real, the two chirsines,
with respecks from his missus, seepy and sewery, and a request might
she passe of him for a minnikin. A call to pay and light a taper, in Brie-
on-Arrosa, back in a sprizzling. The cock striking mine, the stalls bridely
sign, there's Zambosy waiting for Me! She said she wouldn't be half her
length away. Then, then, as soon as the lump his back was turned, with
her mealiebag slang over her shulder, Anna Livia, oysterface, forth of
her bassein came.

The Rivers of Universal History

The washerwomen's action of scrubbing itself takes on a rivery aspect.

my wrists are wrusty rubbing the mouldaw [River Moldau] stains. And the dneepers [River Dnieper] of wet and the gangres [River Ganges] of sin in it.

Joyce deliberately collected river names from all over the world for inclusion in the text because, as he said, he wished in the future that young people reading this section in many different parts of the world would feel at home once they spotted the name of their own river.

ALP's Grief

The last pages of ALP, as twilight gathers, are among the most magically musical Joyce ever wrote. We hear the metallic chime of a clock: "Pingpong! There's the Belle for Sexaloitez! And Concepta de Send-us-pray! Pang!"

A cold wind is blowing over the river and the mood becomes elegiac. Joyce seems to catch the grief of the Irish Diaspora as the dispersal of Anna Livia's children is mourned.

Wharnow are alle her childer, say? In kingdome gone or power to come or gloria be to them farther? Allalivial, allalluvial! Same here, more no more, more again lost alla stranger.

After a flash of lightning, dusk begins to fall. The shapes of the two old washer women blur and solidify as one becomes a tree and the other a stone. Unable to hear each other distinctly but still vaguely murmuring their gossip about the human family while they dissolve into the swirling waters of the night river.

Can't hear with the waters of. The chittering waters of. Flittering bats, fieldmice bawk talk. Ho! Are you not gone ahome? What Thom Malone? Can't hear with bawk of bats, all thim liffeying waters of. Ho, talk save us! My foos won't moos. I feel as old as yonder elm. A tale told of Shaun or Shem? All Livia's daughter-sons. Dark hawks hear us. Night! Night! My ho head halls. I feel as heavy as yonder stone. Tell me of John or Shaun? Who were Shem and Shaun the living sons or daughters of? Night now! Tell me, tell me, tell me, elm! Night night! Telmetale of stem or stone. Beside the rivering waters of, hitherandthithering waters of. Night!

But Anna Livia herself is indestructible in this magical landscape.

Tys Elvenland! Teems of times and happy returns. The seim anew.
Ordovico or viricordo. Anna was, Livia is, Plurabelle's to be.

As Joyce himself wrote to Harriet Weaver . . .

The Exile's Last Exile

The publication of **Finnegans Wake** in 1939 effectively marked the end of Joyce's creative career. As the war clouds gathered, he was once more preoccupied with protecting Lucia. For a year he retired to the country at St Gerand le Puy where he occasionally received old friends like Samuel Beckett and Paul Léon. As the situation worsened with the fall of France and the reality of German occupation, he made a dash for Switzerland where he hoped to find sanctuary as he had in the First World War. He arrived in Zurich with his family in December 1940, a wanderer once more, but he had little strength left and on 13 January 1941 he died following an operation for a perforated duodenal ulcer.

When Joyce left Dublin in 1904 the Provost of Trinity College, the Rev. Sir John Pentland Mahaffy, echoed the sentiments of many of his contemporaries when he said:

Thank God they (Joyce and George Moore) have both cleared out of Dublin. But not before they had squirted stink upon all the decent people like a pair of skunks. James Joyce is a living argument in defence of my contention that it was a mistake to establish a separate university for the Aboriginals of the island.

By now most of the stink has cleared and we can see Joyce for what he actually was – a man devoted to his family and to his art.

Joyce is now even becoming fashionable in his native city (such is the disinfectant power of tourist dollars!) and **Bloomsday** (16 June) is showing signs of becoming a Dublin equivalent of New Orleans' Mardi Gras.

As Mr O'Connor remarked of Parnell in Joyce's **Dubliners**' story "Ivy Day in the Committee Room": "We all respect him – now that he's dead and gone."

A question this most autobiographical of writers might have put to himself is . . .

Further Reading

The works of James Joyce are readily available, for instance, in the Penguin paperback Twentieth-Century Classics which are provided with useful notes.

The best introduction to Joyce and his world is the enthralling and massively detailed biography, **James Joyce** by Richard Ellman, Oxford University Press, 1984. Two other useful critical introductions to Joyce's work are, **Here Comes Everybody: Introduction to James Joyce for the Ordinary Reader** by Anthony Burgess, Arena Books, 1987, and **James Joyce: His Way of Interpreting the Modern World**, by William York Tindall, Greenwood Press, 1979.

Further insight into the mind and family of Joyce may be gained from **Selected Letters**, edited by Richard Ellman, Faber, 1976. It is worth digging out the fascinating memoir by Stanislaus Joyce, **My Brother's Keeper**, Viking Press, 1958.

Other good critical introductions to Joyce are, **Dublin's Joyce**, by Hugh Kenner, Beacon Books, 1962, and, very helpful to the average reader, **A Reader's Guide to James Joyce** by William York Tindall, Thames and Hudson, 1959, out of print but available in good libraries.

For help with **Ulysses**, Stuart Gilbert's early study with his chapter by chapter breakdown, **James Joyce's Ulysses**, Alfred Knopf, 1952, is good but again will require looking up in a library. The same is true of Weldon Thornton's **Allusions in Ulysses**, Chapel Hill, 1968, a page by page annotation of the text which unravels many mysteries. A very engaging view of Joyce and his method of composition will be found in **James Joyce and the Making of Ulysses** by his friend, the Cornish sculptor, Frank Budgen, Oxford University Press, 1989.

A useful introduction to **Finnegans Wake** is the **Shorter Finnegans Wake** edited by Anthony Burgess, Faber, 1966. **A Skeleton Key to Finnegans Wake** by J. Campbell and H.M. Morton, Harcourt, Brace & World, 1944, may take some finding, but it will help the reader "crack" the system. For the enthusiast who wants an almost word by word "translation", try **Annotations to Finnegans Wake** by Roland McHugh, Routledge & Kegan Paul, 1980.

David Norris is Senior Lecturer in English Literature in Trinity College Dublin. He was Chairman of the International James Joyce Symposia of 1977, 1982 and 1992. He is co-editor of the proceedings of the James Joyce International Symposia of 1982 and 1992, Chairman of the James Joyce Cultural Centre in Dublin and Chairman of the North Great George Street Preservation Society. He is a member of the Upper House of the Irish Parliament and a Bureau Member of the Foreign Affairs Committee.

Carl Flint, a true Derbyshire (Chesterfield) lad, has been a regular contributor of illustrations and comic strips to Select, NME, Punch, Deadline, Escape, Red Dwarf, Sonic the Comic and Aquarist and Pondkeeper.

Acknowledgements

Lettering and layout by Woodrow Phoenix.

Thanks to the following people who posed so sportingly as the main characters in this book: David Lyttleton, Jo Anne Smith, Jane Kendrick, Joyce Smith, Keith Petchey, Richard Haigh, Ivan Cotterill, Mitzi Rosette, Chris Webster. The Bricklayers Arms and The Barley Mow provided pub settings. And thanks also to Ed Hillyer and Garry Marshall.

Also recommended by Carl Flint: Minit Classics present Ulysses, a mini-comic strip by David Lasky, Box 181, 4505 University Way, N.E. Seattle, WA 98105, USA. $1 or write for catalogue.

Index